CREATIVE WRITING

Lavonne Mueller
formerly of
DeKalb High School
DeKalb, Illinois

Jerry D. Reynolds
English Consultant
Rochester Public Schools
Rochester, Minnesota

 National Textbook Company
NTC a division of *NTC Publishing Group* • Lincolnwood, Illinois USA

ACKNOWLEDGMENTS

From "I Want to Know Why" from THE TRIUMPH OF THE EGG by Sherwood Anderson, copyright © 1921 by B.W. Heubsch, Inc., renewed 1948 by Eleanor C. Anderson. Reprinted with permission of Harold Ober Associates, Inc./ "The Fun They Had," copyright © 1957 by Isaac Asimov, from the book EARTH IS ROOM ENOUGH by Isaac Asimov. Reprinted with permission of Doubleday & Company, Inc., and N.E.A. Service, Inc./ "The Indian Wants" and from "Paste Pot Poetry" by Norbert Blei. Used by permission of author./ From "Tony's Fluke Day" by Jimmy Breslin. Copyright © 1963 by Jimmy Breslin. Reprinted by permission of The Sterling Lord Agency, Inc./ "Butter Churns" by Laurie Brunson from FOXFIRE 3 edited by Eliot Wigginton, copyright © 1975 by The Foxfire Fund, Inc. Reprinted by permission of Doubleday & Company, Inc./ From "All the Years of Her Life" by Morley Callaghan. Copyright 1935, 1962 by Morley Callaghan, reprinted by permission of Harold Matson Co., Inc./ From IN COLD BLOOD by Truman Capote. Copyright © 1965 by Truman Capote. Reprinted by permission of Random House, Inc./ "The Secret Heart" from COLLECTED POEMS by Robert P. Tristram Coffin. Copyright 1935 by Macmillan Publishing Co., Inc., renewed 1963 by Margaret Coffin Halvosa. Reprinted with permission of Macmillan Publishing Co., Inc./ From SLOUCHING TOWARDS BETHLEHEM by Joan Didion, copyright © 1966, 1968 by Joan Didion. Reprinted with the permission of Farrar, Straus & Giroux, Inc./ Annotations for THE CRUCIBLE by Arthur Miller prepared by David Dwight and used courtesy of David Dwight./ "My Shoes" by Karl Elder. Used by permission of author and FOLIO./ From "Take the Plunge" by Gloria Emerson, reprinted by permission of International Creative Management, copyright © 1976 by Gloria Emerson. First published in *Esquire Magazine*./ From "World's Most Amazing Device Has 1,001 Uses" by Robert

(ACKNOWLEDGMENTS continued on page 256.)

1992 Printing

This edition first published in 1990 by National Textbook Company,
a division of NTC Publishing Group.
© 1990, 1977 by NTC Publishing Group,
4255 West Touhy Avenue, Lincolnwood (Chicago), Illinois 60646-1975 U.S.A.
Originally published by Laidlaw Brothers, Publishers.
Library of Congress Card Catalog Number: 89-62133
Manufactured in the United States of America
2 3 4 5 6 7 8 9 VP 9 8 7 6 5 4 3

CONTENTS

1. THE WRITER'S JOURNAL

why write?

You wouldn't be reading this if you weren't interested in writing. Maybe you're interested because of a story you read—you felt *you'd* like to write something like that. Maybe you're just curious. Or maybe you've got something you want to say and you're not sure how to say it. Whatever your reason, you're reading this because you're interested in writing.

The writers portrayed on TV and in the movies never seem to work. They dash off great novels and scripts for hit plays in the wink of an eye. They have brilliant ideas constantly—they never have to sit down and really think. Most of their time is devoted to going to parties in penthouses and on yachts. It all looks very easy. And fun, too. But

> **There's not much doubt in any of our minds that no complete idea springs fully formed from our brow, needing only a handshake and a signature on the contract to send it off into the world to make twenty-five billion dollars. The germ of the idea grows very slowly . . .**

So said the late cartoonist and writer Walt Kelly. And if you don't believe him, take a look at this. It's a paragraph from an article by Ernest Hemingway. At the time it was written, it was just another paragraph, but the events it described contained what Kelly called "the germ of the idea."

> Another time an old man fishing alone in a skiff out of Cabañas hooked a great marlin that, on the heavy sash-cord handline, pulled the skiff far out to sea. Two days later the old man was picked up by fishermen sixty miles to the eastward, the head and forward part of the marlin lashed alongside. What was left of the fish, less than half, weighed eight hundred pounds. The old man had stayed with him a day, a night, a day and another night while the fish swam deep and pulled the boat. When he had come up the old man had pulled the boat up on him and harpooned him. Lashed alongside the sharks had hit him and the old man had fought them out alone in the Gulf Stream in a skiff, clubbing them, stabbing at them, lung-

ing at them with an oar until he was exhausted and the sharks had eaten all that they could hold. He was crying in the boat when the fishermen picked him up, half crazy from his loss, and the sharks were still circling the boat.

Eighteen years later, this germ had grown to become *The Old Man and the Sea*, a novel that helped Hemingway win the Nobel prize for literature.

how the pros do it

Professional writers, like Ernest Hemingway, don't dash off their masterpieces. They take their time. They build carefully. And even for them, good ideas are hard to come by. Professional writers are the real misers of this world. They waste nothing. Like magpies, they are crazy collectors. They hoard scraps of conversation, wise-cracks, bits of odd information, pieces of description, curious combinations of words—everything.

you never know

Professional writers keep journals. It's their ace in the hole, their Swiss bank account. They know the terror of facing a blank sheet of paper empty-handed or empty-headed. That's why they keep journals. A journal is something to fall back on when the going gets rough. A writer without a journal has no place to store promising ideas, no private place in which to think with a pencil.

so what's a journal?

When someone says "journal," maybe you think of a leather-bound volume with blue-lined pages. Some writers use such things. But others write on paper bags with ball-point pens. For many writers, their journal consists of desk drawers stuffed with scraps of paper. A journal is whatever you say it is—so long as you can easily get to what's in it.

SETTING UP YOUR JOURNAL

1. Decide what you'd like your journal to look like. Will it be a loose-leaf notebook, a file box, an accordion file, a large brown envelope? Or a design of your own? Go to a discount store or an office supply store and buy the materials you'll need. Also buy something to write with, if you don't have it already.
2. Give your journal a title. The title will be the first really creative thing you'll do for your journal, so make your title witty, unusual, thought provoking.
3. You may wish to decorate the cover of your journal. You could sketch on the cover, paste on an advertisement or a photo, or write your favorite quotes on it.

So now you've decided what your journal will look like. Now you may wonder . . .

what goes into my journal?

What interests you? Write about that. About your crazy friend Susan's latest practical joke. Or the night at camp when you heard weird noises outside the tent. Or your first date. Or your seventy-two-year-old grandmother with her young ideas. Write these things down. If they mean something to you, chances are they'll mean something to someone else and will make good material for a story or poem. For example, James Baldwin used his memories of his preacher father for a long essay in *Notes of a Native Son*.

What else can go into your journal? Jack Kerouac used a journal to record progress on his novel *On the Road*, a 1957 classic of the "beat generation." Professionals use journals for all sorts of things. They jot down . . .

observations

Writers look everywhere. And they collect what they see—in descriptions in their journals. Then, later, they write about telephone poles, plums, skyscrapers, people's feet, computers, sky divers, neon signs, an old woman waiting for a bus—anything and everything they've observed. What interesting, unusual, even startling things can you describe in your journal? Perhaps you're intrigued by an electric pencil sharpener that gobbles pencils, a small girl walking a Great Dane, the 747 you saw at the airport, one flower growing in a front yard full of weeds. Describe these things in your journal. Chances are, you'll use some of these descriptions later in your poems or stories.

Another important thing to include in your journal is your . . .

imaginings

Imagination is the stuff that poems, plays, and stories are made of. When she was a girl, Gwendolyn Brooks, the Pulitzer prize-winning poet, filled many notebooks with poems about the patterns she saw in the clouds. In the same way, you can use your imagination on the world around you. Imagine patterns in the clouds or in the stars. Or you may notice a woman sitting on the bus who's carrying a toolbox. Can you imagine where she's going? The job she has? What she's thinking? Try writing a mini-biography about her. Hoard it for later.

12

John Kerouac
1948-'49

Journal during first stages of "On the Road" (B.S. Smith)

MONDAY NOV. 29 — That's 32,500-words
since I started on Nov. 9, or better than
1500 words per day... per sitting, very high.
Altho this is only the first draft, and I still
have no idea where I'm heading with it, I
delight in the figures, as always, because
they are concrete evidence of a greater
freedom in writing than I had in Town &
City. However, who knows about the qual-
ity? I have been sitting down & writing
with perfect equanimity, and I hope I
can go on like this from now on and write
a great many good books all intertwined.
Still — lately — I've had a feeling of emptiness... not boredom, just emptiness & even
falseness. These are not the reverent, mad
feelings during Town & City, altho I'm con-
vinced it indicates "artistic" growth; as
for "spiritual growth," I can't say at all...
yet. My whole feeling & knowledge now
is concentrated on people, and not beyond
them in the realms of "spirituality" — (I
do believe.) So a new notebook (the other
one was sloppy to write in due to the
bulge of the pages.) This is better. These
absurd little interests in notebook-paper
are connected with the gravity of early
boyhood diaries. We need our petit ab-
sorptions like campstools in the wilderness.
(How neat.) Tonight wrote 1500-words
good ones too. To bed reading anthropology.
TUESDAY NOV. 30 — No news from Little, Brown yet.
Wrote 1000-words in the afternoon. A

13

What else can you include?

dreams

Many writers include their dreams in their journals. The American poet Diane Wakoski used her journal to record a series of dreams that were like episodes in a story. Record a dream you had last night or an exciting dream you can't forget. Perhaps your dream will give you an idea. Or perhaps—like some writers—you'll use an actual dream in a poem or story.

Camerique

Anything else you can include in your journal?

sketches, doodles, cartoons

Make your journal fun to look at. Try sketching your friends, the front of your classroom, or an interesting object like a movie projector. Doodle. Or create a cartoon—about yourself, your family, or your school. The novelist Flannery O'Connor, for example, used to make cartoons and sketches in her notebook.

ads, photos, newspaper clippings

Collect these—the interesting ones, the ones that strike you as unusual and different—and paste them in your journal. These, too, may give you ideas.

Pink cells help calm prisoners

SAN JOSE, Cal. [UPI]—A police officer at the Santa Clara County jail credits a pink paint job in one of the holding cells with reducing the number of fights in the unit by about one-third.

Capt. Mike Miller said he has found that pink has a "calming influence" on the prisoners. He said since the holding pen was painted pink, the number of fights among prisoners has declined by 30 to 40 percent.

Miller said he was so impressed with the color theory that he has started replacing the cells' traditional green with a subdued yellow, which he says is even better than pink, because its tranquilizing effect lasts longer.

and much, much more

Write about and collect whatever interests you. With so many things in your journal, you won't have to face a blank sheet of paper alone.

there's a bonus

In addition to a journal's being a storehouse, it's also a good place to practice writing. MacKinlay Kantor, an American novelist, said this about practicing writing:

> **There is a mystery about stringing words together which cannot well be solved until one has strung a lot of words together.**

Edith Sitwell, an English poet and prose writer, also practiced in her journal. She says that she practiced writing the way a pianist practices music. Pianists, of course, don't *start* with Beethoven or even Scott Joplin—instead they warm up with finger exercises. Later, they can play the difficult because they've warmed up on something simple. This is the bonus. By the time you're ready for a poem or story, you've already improved your writing because you've practiced in your journal.

July 17

Idea for story – experience at swimming pool. Man who wouldn't let us in. All I can ~~see or~~ remember about his face is his gold tooth glaring at me – gold tooth gold, not pretty gold, dull – Some people are rich enough to have gold in their teeth –

I never saw the man's eyes. ~~In fact I don't remember anything about him except~~

Just his mouth. ~~with its~~ He had a gold tooth in front and I remembered it wasn't pretty like most gold but ~~kinda kind of~~ kinda dull and brassy looking. That tooth just seemed to glare at me and I knew that he was saying ~~that we couldn't~~ "no" cause we had no place in his pool or any pool where people had gold in their teeth.

one very important question

You may ask, "Why collect all this? Why store dreams and descriptions, puns and phrases, memories and imaginings, first attempts?" The answer is that if you don't store these things, you'll lose them. They won't be there when you need them.

a second very important question

How much is enough? The answer is that you'll need more than you can use. Look through any writer's journal and you'll see many items that never made it—never became stories or poems or plays. When he first heard and jotted down the story about the fisherman, Hemingway couldn't be sure he'd be able to use it. And that's the problem. You can never be sure what you'll need. So you'd better have more than enough.

where do you go from here?

Now you may wonder, "How do I go about writing in my journal? Writing sounds *hard*." Professional writers will tell you that writing *is* often hard. So the pros set up a writing routine. Most of them write at the same time and in the same place every day. This way, writing becomes a habit. And habit makes everything easier.

In setting up your routine, you should consider . . .

when to write

Some writers can't get their ideas flowing until the evening. They may write far into the night. For example, George S. Kaufman, a famous Broadway playwright, couldn't sleep at night, so he used writing to fill the sleepless hours until dawn. Others may start writing at four in the morning. They wouldn't dream of washing dishes or going to the office until they've finished writing. Still others may prefer to begin writing at high noon.

What's the best time to do your personal writing? Early morning? Noon? Five in the afternoon? Experiment to find the best time. Then stick to it.

Also consider . . .

where to write

> [My writing table] has seen all my wretchedness, knows all my plans, has overheard all my thoughts.
> —Honoré de Balzac

Most professionals write in the same place every day. Maybe they write at the kitchen table, in the basement, in their study, or on the bus. Experiment to find a place where you can be alone. If people keep coming and going through the room or the TV is always on, you may find it hard to concentrate.

what you write with

This is important. It's part of your writing routine. But don't writers use a pencil or a typewriter? Or a personal computer? Not always.

> **I used my daughter's crayons for each main character. One end of the wallpaper was the beginning of the story, and the other end was the end, and then there was all that middle part, which was the middle.**
>
> **—Kurt Vonnegut, Jr.**

Writers have even used felt-tip markers to write with. Use whatever you like. Just be sure you can read what you write.

be comfortable

Writers like to wear comfortable clothing while they write—it helps put them in the mood. The Russian novelist Tolstoy liked to write in a peasant shirt. The French novelist Balzac wrote in a dressing gown. When you're writing at home, choose comfortable clothing, something that makes you feel like a writer. Many writers are most comfortable sitting at a desk. But some prefer to write lying down, or standing up. Others prefer to slouch in a comfortable chair and use a lapboard to hold their writing. Truman Capote often wrote stretched out on a couch or in a hammock. Hemingway used to like to write standing up at a lectern.

finally, some tricks

Writers use little tricks to get themselves in the mood for writing, to get their ideas flowing. Anne Sexton, an American poet, wrote

**I think of myself as writing for one person,
that one perfect reader who understands and loves.**

She found that she wrote better if she imagined the perfect audience. Perhaps this will work for you. Imagine your perfect audience—a friend, a teacher, someone sympathetic, patient, friendly, interested.

Other writers, like the French novelist Françoise Sagan, enjoy listening to music while they write. Try listening to different kinds of music—rock, folk, classical—while you write. Does this work for you?

Sometimes writers are inspired by art. Gertrude Stein, for example, said that her book *Three Lives* was inspired by a painting by Cézanne. Check out an art book from the library and study the pictures. Or visit an art museum. Do the paintings give you ideas for writing?

Perhaps you can discover some tricks of your own. Things that help you write better, that make writing easier.

So now you'd like to get started on your journal. Start by going through the following checklist.

SETTING UP YOUR WRITING ROUTINE

1. Try writing at several different times until you find the one you like best. Then try always to write at that time.

2. Try writing in several different places. If you choose your room, perhaps you could put a big sheet of poster board on the wall or set up a bulletin board. On either of these, you could post your most successful writing. You could also tape up cards with some of your favorite quotes.

3. If you're writing at home, put on some comfortable clothes.

4. Try listening to music while you write. Or study some paintings. Do either of these help get you in the mood to write? What works for you?

2. GETTING STARTED, KEEPING GOING

warm-ups

You've designed your journal, given it a catchy title. Now you're ready to make your first entry. What will it be? To help you get started now and to keep you going later, here's something really different. It's a grab bag of warm-ups. What's a warm-up? A warm-up is an idea starter, a mind jogger, something to help you write when you run out of ideas or just can't get started. Sooner or later this happens to every writer. When it happens to you, turn to this section and do one or more of these warm-ups in your journal. The warm-ups will help you get going, and they may give you ideas for later use. They include practice in many of the things a writer needs to know—how to create dialogue, sketch a character, choose and use words effectively. The warm-ups also suggest places to find ideas—like newspapers, paintings and drawings, proverbs, quotations, photos. Use these warm-ups whenever you're in need of an idea. And stockpile them in your journal, even though they don't seem very useful at the time. You can come back to them again and again.

anagrams

Developing curiosity about words and letters, manipulating them, playing word games—all help to keep a writer's feel for words well oiled and ready for use. Take some words, rearrange the letters, and see whether you can make new words out of them. For example, the letters in the phrase *French Revolution* can be re-arranged to spell "violence run forth." The letters in the name *Florence Nightingale* can be used to spell "flit on, cheering angel." These rearrangements are called *anagrams*. Anagrams are often used by writers to conceal real names or to give the reader a puzzle to unravel. Look at the following anagrams. Then try writing some of your own.

rebate   beater

the eyes   they see

mood time   emit doom

You might also try coining a pen name by making an anagram of your real name.

Paul Peterson   Pete R. Paulson

Or try an anagram poem. Notice that the first letters of the lines combine to spell the subject of the poem.

> Let's sit for a while and simply talk
> Of you and me,
> Very softly, using
> Eyes as well as words.

time capsule

Suppose you were asked to prepare a time capsule. You are going to put into this capsule items that would tell future ages what life was like in your own time. What would you include? In California, a time capsule contained not only newspapers and financial reports but motion pictures and a football that was used by the Los Angeles Rams. For a writer, being aware of characteristic signs of the times is essential. How aware are you of your world? Here is a list of time-capsule items suggested by a high-school class in Illinois. Jot down in your journal items you would include in a capsule to be opened in 300 years.

A bag of microwave popcorn
A Baby on Board car sign
A love letter from Jennifer to Michael
A tamper-proof package
An erasable pen
A stick of sugarless gum
A pair of sweatpants
A bottle of polluted water
Steffi Graf's tennis racket
An empty box of oatbran cereal
A set of ankle weights
An instant replay of a commercial for a new, improved paper towel
A copy of *People* magazine
A copy of *USA Today*

A empty carton of lo-cal yogurt
A poster for a rock band
A pair of running shoes
A UPC (Universal Product Code) symbol on a bread wrapper
A can of Diet Cherry 7UP
A microchip
A rock music videotape
A Walkman
A compact disk
A cash-register receipt for a loaf of bread and a quart of milk
A Nintendo game

story fill-in

Here's an incomplete story about a UFO—an unidentified flying object—for you to finish. Use your imagination and inventiveness to fill in the blanks. Whether your story ends up being a humorous farce or a serious science-fiction tale depends upon the words you choose. By filling in the blanks and completing the story, you'll be experimenting with word choice and learning how words interact with one another.

In writing stories, you'll discover that the words you choose for the beginning often determine the words you use later. For example, if you decide to spoof science-fiction stories by making your UFO a flying pancake, then you must choose words that consistently maintain humor and fantasy.

Sometimes word choice may work the other way around. After you've begun, you may decide that instead of a deserted woods you want a crowd of curious bystanders in your story. Then you'll have to go back and choose words that change your setting to something like a busy street or crowded shopping center.

Copy the story, including the blanks, into your journal. Then fill in the blanks with words that create a consistent tone and mood throughout the story. Later you may want to create your own incomplete story, leaving blanks for word choices. Give the story to two different classmates to complete. Compare the two versions. Store them in your journal.

I Saw a UFO

Late one afternoon I was —ing through —. I crossed the — and entered —. Twilight had come, and it was very — there. All at once, I heard —. I looked up, and there was a — coming straight down. It landed with a —. I was —! "I'm seeing a —!" I thought.

I — closer. I tried to touch the — with my —, but my — bounced off a — that surrounded the UFO. Then a — opened in its side. A — was lowered. Out came a —. It had a — like that of a —. In two of its hands it carried a machine that looked like a —. I think it took my —. Then the — was taken up again. There was a — and the UFO shot up —. Then it changed course and hovered over —. Suddenly, it was gone! On the ground where it had been was a —. I — home and told my neighbors about the —. They said, "—! You've been reading too many —!" But I decided to report the UFO to —.

Moral: Don't go — in —, or you may have your — taken by a — from —.

29

chance poetry

One theory of art is that the creative person should create in the same chance manner that nature itself does—like the random scattering of wild flowers and rocks that make a beautiful scene. Tristan Tzara, a poet who put this theory into practice, created poems by picking words from a hat.

Perhaps chance does play a part in coming up with just the right combination of words. But you need judgment to recognize that the combination is right. You might like to try your luck and test your judgment with some chance poetry. Cut out words from headlines or ads. Put all the "cut" words into a small box. Shake the box and pull out the words one by one. Record each word as you go along. Now look over your poem. What has chance given you? Something like this?

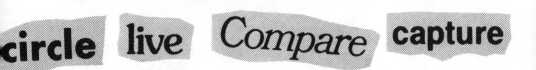

Can you find any interesting phrases in your chance "poem" that give you an idea for a story, or that you might use in writing a new poem?

dialogue between opposites

Dialogue is essential to fiction. It's the essence of drama and often of short stories and novels as well. Here's your chance to practice writing some dialogue—and to use your imagination.

Write a dialogue between two completely opposite types of people. You might, for example, have Ann Landers and Sigmund Freud discuss psychology. Or have Charlie Brown ask advice of Dennis the Menace. Or have an astronaut and a being from another planet compare life in their respective worlds. Write your dialogue in the form of a script, but without description or narrative. Your dialogue may be humorous or serious or both. Decide just how the conversation would go. What would these people say to each other? Could they find anything in common? What questions might they ask each other? What favors might they ask each other?

Before you begin, read the following imagined dialogue between Madonna and Beethoven.

> BEETHOVEN: *Fräulein,* your concert was *wunderbar!* But music certainly has changed. Forgive me. Let me introduce myself. My name is Beethoven, and I've been traveling through the centuries, finding out what's happening to music.
>
> MADONNA: Beethoven. Like *the* Beethoven?
>
> BEETHOVEN: *Ja, the* Beethoven, Ludwig van.
>
> MADONNA: Way cool! Say, I admire your garb.
>
> BEETHOVEN: *Danke schön* . . . Uh, whatever you said. This kind of music you make. It is called . . . ?
>
> MADONNA: Pop rock.
>
> BEETHOVEN: "Rock" as in stones?
>
> MADONNA: Like in Rolling Stones.
>
> BEETHOVEN: I must admit, this all seems a little strange to me. In *my* day we wore coat and tails to concerts . . . or elegant dresses. No ripped pants and black leather jackets.
>
> MADONNA: Well, it's supercool to keep up with the fashions. The audience really goes mad over the styles.

BEETHOVEN: About the music. I always preferred *planned* emotion, note by note. I even plan the silences between notes. I worked and worked on the beginning of my fifth symphony. Every note had to be perfect.

MADONNA: We're more into the groove and the beat. I like my music to be spontaneous. We couldn't call yours spontaneous, then.

BEETHOVEN: Maybe not. But there's bad spontaneous as well as good spontaneous, isn't there?

MADONNA: That's right, babe. Lots of rhythm and beat. Just let go and dance your heart out.

BEETHOVEN: You know, music these days isn't too bad. I suppose I needn't have worried. But I *still* think you should dress formally for a concert, and no yelling. Bad for the voice.

MADONNA: Well, babe, it's just a new age.

reacting to a newspaper article

Newspapers and magazines are often good sources for ideas. When you're stuck, they're a good place to turn.

Read the following. It's part of a feature story taken from a newspaper.

One office girl spent almost four months fashioning paper clips into a 40-pound dress she wore at a trade show in McCormick Place.

It was one of the more bizarre uses for paper clips, but not particularly surprising in view of the myriad ways in which people use the familiar device.

In 1958, Lloyd's Bank of London followed the lifetime of 100,000 paper clips and found that only 20,000 ended up holding papers together.

Another 14,163 were twisted and bent during phone conversations; 19,143 were used as chips in card games;

7,200 were pressed into service as "makeshift hooks on women's undergarments"; 5,434 became toothpicks or ear scratchers; 5,308 became nail cleaners; 3,916 were used as pipe cleaners; and the rest, almost 25,000, were simply dropped on the floor and swept away.

But paper clip dresses and pipe cleaners may be a thing of the past. Today there is a shortage of paper clips, creating a crisis so critical that top bureaucrats in Washington are seeking ways to increase the supply.

—*Robert Enstad*

Now read this poem based on the feature story. Perhaps you could write a poem like this.

MISSING: THE REMEDY FOR EVERYTHING

What will we do now?
We're running out of paper clips!
Why, how can I

> make instant sculpture
> and chain necklaces
> and any number of
> silvery odds and ends
> without paper clips?

How can I
clip off an hour of time
by fooling with a paper clip?
How can I
run at a great clip with . . .
no paper clips!
And if the world gets tired,
begins to fall apart,
I was hoping
to clip it back together . . .
with paper clips.
So what shall we do?

The poem you've just read responds to the humorous tone of the article by making puns on the word *clip* and by proposing a humorous solution to the world's problems. There are other ways to respond to the article. You might write a fantasy about why the paper clips are disappearing. Or a story about an unusual use for paper clips. Or a humorous story about how the administration in Washington went into a flutter over the famous paper-clip crisis.

Look through a newspaper or magazine for interesting news or human-interest items. Choose the one you like best and use it as the basis for a story or poem.

writing about pictures

Sometimes you can get ideas for stories or poems by looking at pictures. Study the drawing by Käthe Kollwitz. Look at the three people in her drawing. How old do you think each is? Do you think they're related? What does each person seem to be feeling? The title of the drawing is "Listening." If the picture were unlabeled, could you tell what the people are doing? How? What might they

be listening to or for? Is something about to happen? Is the something good or bad? What might each be thinking?

Now write your response to the drawing. There are many ways to interpret it. Perhaps you think the three persons' expressions do not show fear, but wonder and expectation. Could you write a brief fantasy in which they are waiting for something wonderful, but a little frightening, to happen? Or might they be characters in a mystery story, listening to an eerie sound? What sound might they hear? What might be going to happen?

Or instead of a response, try to do with words what the artist did with charcoal. Describe these people so that the reader can "see" their faces, their attitude, their physical relationship.

Maybe this drawing doesn't suggest anything to you. All right. Try something different. Look at this drawing by Tanya Joyce.

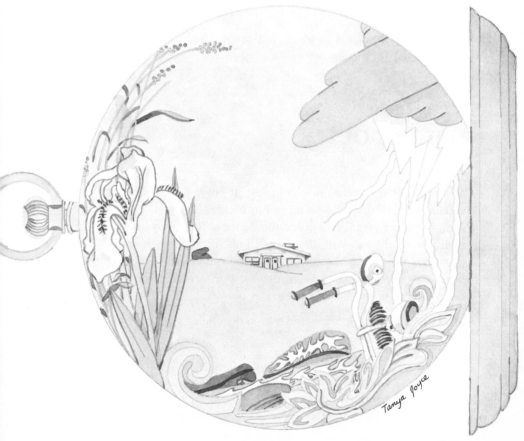

Here's what she has to say about her drawing.

> My sketch shows a new house on the edge of the land.
> Is there a housing tract over the horizon? Has a farmer
> sold his land and moved on? Whose motorcycle is parked
> by the road close to the spectator in the painting? Does
> the bike belong to one of us? Iris and wheat are images
> of quiet beauty and endurance to me. Clouds and light-
> ning are images of fear and a wild, exciting kind of
> beauty at the same time. It is hard for me to say why I
> painted all these images inside the case of a pocket watch
> except that I believe all these images are related to *time*.
> I also remember some novel which I can't name, and in
> this book a man treasured his father's pocket watch.

Write a poem or story about this drawing. How does this scene
make you feel? Is there a tone of sadness surrounding the drawing? Try to describe the different objects in their relationship to
time.

You might also collect pictures that catch your eye. Store them in
your journal for future reference.

name poetry

Many poets like to write rhymed verse. It poses a challenge, teaches
certain kinds of discipline, and is fun besides. Try your hand at the
simple rhymed verse form called the clerihew. It's a four-line poem in
which line 1 rhymes with line 2, and line 3 rhymes with line 4. The
poem has no regular rhythm. It contains a humorous reference to a
famous person. The last line contains a pun, usually on some well-
known event in the life of the famous person.

Read the following clerihew and then write one or more of your own.

> The wind blew chill.
> Many were ill.
> But still our George
> Didn't get cold feet at Valley Forge.

You might also like to try writing a *name limerick*. It's a five-line poem in which lines 1, 2, and 5 rhyme and lines 3 and 4 rhyme. Its rhythm is regular, and the last line must contain a well-known person's name.

> There was a very old uncle,
> Whose guitar went plink and bar-runkle,
> But he said: "I don't care,
> If my music's not fair;
> I know I'm no Simon & Garfunkel."

performance art

Performance art is an expression of creativity through drama, visual art, music, dance, or through a multi-media approach. Performance art can happen anywhere—at a gallery, in a museum, at a nightclub, or on a theatre stage lit with a single light. It can be a man delivering a rambling monologue, with posters in the background, or a woman telling a story, using props she pulls from an old trunk. To define performance art, one artist used the following analogy: performance art is to the theatre what poetry is to prose. Following are three examples of performance art. The first was actually staged in Chicago, the second was conceived and performed by members of a visual and performing arts class, and the third was "designed" by a creative writing student.

STORE WINDOW

Two performing artists make an arrangement with a store to sit in the front window all night. They sit at a card table with a microphone, talking, and taking notes. Passersby stop and stare, listening to the dialogue coming out of the outside speaker.

INCIDENT IN THE PARK

Two young men walk through a park, each carrying a bag of groceries. Each wears a hat. Suddenly, as they pass each other, they set their bags down, pull out oranges, and start juggling—first independently, then with each other—humming a circus tune. They suddenly stop, repack their bags, and continue on their way.

The houselights of the theater dim. A table is spot-lighted on center stage. A man wearing an apron and with a baby carrier strapped to his back approaches the table. There is a doll in the baby carrier. On the table is a carton of eggs and a large bowl. Dramatically, but carefully, the man removes an egg from the carton, cracks it in the bowl, and replaces the empty shells in the carton. He repeats the process twelve times until all the eggs are cracked. Then he takes a pair of cracked egg-shells, scoops some liquid egg from the bowl, and replaces the shells in the carton. He repeats this process twelve times until all the eggs, cracked and dripping, are back in the carton. When he is finished, the spotlight shifts to the doll in the baby carrier, who screams for one minute. Then silence. Then the lights go out.

Now try writing your own example of performance art. Let your imagination run free. Don't worry about being logical. Performance art has the logic of a dream.

familiar opening lines

What kind of person would open a conversation like this, "You know I hate to gossip, but . . ."? Can you see this person in your mind? Would you trust him or her? Opening lines can often tell a great deal about a person. Here are some familiar opening lines compiled by a group of students. Add some other lines to the list. Be ready to imagine and then to describe the kind of person who might say each of these lines. You might also like to complete the lines.

For example, a parent or teacher might begin, "If I've told you once, I've told you . . ." Suppose you decide the speaker is a parent, an irritated mother trying to get some sleep. You might finish the line like this:

> If I've told you once, I've told you a thousand times not to play rock records at one in the morning!

Jotting down familiar opening lines in your journal—and adding some replies—is good practice for writing dialogue. Try to match the words of the opening to the personality of the character you imagine saying them.

How do you expect me . . .
I can remember when . . .
You won't believe this, but . . .
A funny thing happened . . .
If there's one thing I can't stand . . .
My fellow Americans . . .
Did it ever occur to you that . . .
It's nothing serious, but . . .
I really shouldn't tell this to anybody, but . . .
There will be a short assignment over the weekend . . .
I hate to criticize anyone, but . . .
Say, you're new around here, aren't you?

weird invitations

Every writer needs a well-developed sense of humor. Here's a chance to use yours by writing funny invitations in your journal. In writing these invitations, you'll also be using satire—you'll be poking fun at people, things, ideas.

For example, the invitation that follows pokes fun at spies and their activities. The society mentioned here is so secret that its members don't even know when or where to meet!

Here's another invitation. This one pokes fun at legends and sports contests.

Sir Terrible Dragon
kindly invites you to witness a contest
between himself and one St. George
Place: A rocky crag
Time: 303 A.D., around sunset

sound words

The pronunciations of some words—like *boom*, *hiss*, and *buzz*—echo their meanings. Such words are said to be onomatopoeic. Some writers have felt it necessary to invent words when none existed to describe a sound they wanted to describe. James Joyce, for example, made up the following word. It's a word that suggests what a thunderstorm sounds like:

bababadalgharaghtakamminarronkonnbronntonnerronn-
tuounnthunntrovarrhounawnskawntoohoohoordenenthurnuk!

Here are some sound words suggested by students:

mullunk (book falling on the floor)
sweshhhhhhhhhhhhheeeee (soft wind in the bushes)
bompth . . . bompth . . . bompth (hammer on wood)
splooooooob, splooooooob (eating oatmeal)

Now make up your own sound words for the following:

A waterfall
Leather heels on brick
Fingernail on the chalkboard
A cat walking across piano keys
Eggs frying
Hail falling against the window
A caterpillar walking on silk cloth
An alarm-clock bell
Grass growing

doodle chart

Doodles are fun to draw. They can also tell a lot about the person who draws them.

The following doodle chart was drawn by a student. Can you put together the girl's doodles and come up with a general idea of what she's like? It's details such as these—as shown in the doodles —that can make a character in a story seem real.

Make a doodle chart of yourself in your journal. Sketch some basic things in your life and label them. From your doodle chart, others should be able to get a general idea of what you're like. You might also like to try putting together doodle charts of people you know.

likes and dislikes

Looked at one way, nearly every piece of writing is a list of likes and dislikes—the reflection of a writer's personal reaction to the world. What makes one poem or essay different from another is that each writer is a unique mixture of likes and dislikes. So why not explore your likes and dislikes? List some of them in your journal, making one column of your likes, another of your dislikes. For example, perhaps you like hot fudge on vanilla ice cream, old Beatles records, antique cars with big grilles and lots of headlamps, travel posters. Perhaps you dislike cold bathroom floors in the morning, sarcastic teachers, wet shoes, directions that are wrong, rice pudding.

There are two things you could do with your lists. You could write a "list-poem." Give your poem a title like "These Things I Like" and arrange the items you like under it. Or a title like "These Things I Hate" and list your dislikes under it. Or you could zero in on some of the items on one of your lists. Perhaps there are a number of items on your list that seem to be about the same general subject. For example, perhaps a number of "likes" about the city. Then you might write a few paragraphs of description or a poem like this:

City Things I Like

The city's full of characters.
Looming grey buildings
have staring eyes
and grinning stone gargoyles
watch on top.

The little bronze girl
in the park fountain
just stands there forever
getting wet.

& pigeons swirl
and flutter
descending like peace
on the quiet park.

A businessman wears
a brown tweed suit
& strides a brisk stride.

& an old woman
walks so slowly:
the street's so long to her,
the curb's so high.

& two lovers don't know
if it's five or noon
(they have each other).

I like the city
because it's full of characters.
It's more real than TV.
                    —*Mary Kelly*

Keep your list alive. Make it grow by adding items as you find new likes and dislikes.

proverbs and quotations

Proverbs and quotations, when they are good, pack a lot of meaning into a few words. Take this Chinese proverb, for example:

> When a finger points at the moon, an imbecile looks at the finger.

You might have to read it twice to be sure you know what it means. Roughly speaking, it means that there are some dull-minded people who are incapable of seeing beauty—in this case, the moon—even when it is shown to them. Instead, they focus on the irrelevant— the pointed finger. Does this idea suggest anything to you? Could you write an essay, a story, or a poem illustrating this idea? You might like to try. Perhaps you could write a humorous story about someone who visits a museum and admires the ventilator grilles instead of the paintings. Or a poem about something beautiful— the glint of winter sunlight on an iron railing—that nobody else seems to notice.

If you prefer, try one of the following. First, ask yourself what the proverb or quotation means. Then experiment. Try using it as the basis of a brief poem, essay, or story.

> You grow up the day you have the first real laugh—at yourself. —*Ethel Barrymore*

> Knowledge is the source of all mystery. —*Shen-hui*

> Too much sunshine makes a desert. —*Arabian proverb*

> It is better to break one's heart than to do nothing with it. —*Margaret Kennedy*

> Quickly got, quickly lost. —*Yiddish proverb*

> Regret is an appalling waste of energy; you can't build on it; it's only good for wallowing in. —*Katherine Mansfield*

public versus private

As a writer you should be aware that people often don't say what they're really thinking. This knowledge can be useful when you're creating characters in a story. To sharpen your awareness of the gap between the public word and the private thought, read the following contrasts written by students. The first line shows what the person says, and the second what the person is thinking. Try to create several contrasts of your own.

How have you been?
  (I can't think of anything to say.)

Did you have fun at Beth's party?
  (I hope you had a terrible time, because I wasn't invited.)

Do you have a ride home?
  (*I* need a ride.)

You have a cute cat here.
  (Would you please get it off me? It scratches.)

Sure, Lucy, I'll be glad to come over and help you with math.
  (I can't stand you, but your brother's real cute.)

How is Spanish?
  (Are you still flunking?)

writing from photos

Sometimes a photograph can be a good source for ideas. A photo can suggest characters, plots, settings, the images for a poem.

Look over the photographs on the following pages. Pick one you like. Study it carefully. Be ready to write a description of it after you've read the suggestions on page 48.

Rohn Engh

Herbert Lanks from A. Devaney, Inc.

Laurence Risser

First of all, can you give the photo a title? If you can't, try describing what's going on in the photo.

If the photo has more than one person in it, try making up some dialogue. Notice facial expressions, gestures, postures. What might each person be feeling? Thinking? Try making up a mini-biography for each.

Is there some kind of conflict in the photo, some tension between people? What, if anything, do you think is going to happen next? What happened just before the photo was taken?

Notice the background in the photo. Sometimes backgrounds can suggest a story plot or how a person might be feeling. For example, why is the boy in the first photo all by himself in the gym? Why are all those chairs set up? Are other people coming, or have they already left?

Perhaps the photo has given you an idea for a poem or a story. Try writing your poem or story in your journal. Or perhaps the photo gave you ideas for characters, a setting, a conflict. Jot down these ideas.

You might also collect some intriguing photos from magazines and newspapers. Paste these photos in your journal. Come back to them when you need ideas.

fantasies with words

Writers love to play with words. One way to have fun with words is to have words act out their meanings. Here's a drawing by Steinberg which does just that—the word *help* is falling off a wall and really needs help!

Copyright © 1954 by Saul Steinberg

See if you can create word pictures like these. For example, you might show the word *sigh* getting smaller and dribbling into a puddle, the word *ouch* with its letters bumping each other, the word *shout* coming from a megaphone and getting larger as it comes out. These are only a few of the many words which could act out their meanings.

writing about clothes

What people wear tells a lot about them. When you create characters for a story, it's important to describe what they're wearing.

Some writers like to write about their own clothing. In doing so, they usually reveal something about themselves. Here's Karl Elder writing about his shoes:

My Shoes

Like 2 mouths,
One comic,
The other sideways
In a frown.
They lay in the dark
Ready for the dawn
To swallow what keeps me up
In a play of putting them on.

In this poem, Elder writes about shoes that are so much a part of him that they seem nearly alive. Somehow the reader is able to see Elder's personality reflected in the poem. Like the shoes, Elder is part sad, part comic.

Now, describe some clothes or other personal objects that you particularly like. In describing them, you'll find that you're revealing a lot about yourself.

You might also like to choose persons in different occupations—a doctor, a taxi driver, a salesperson, a construction worker—and describe how they might be dressed. You'll need details like these when you create characters in a story.

writing about food

Through the ages, writers and artists have been fascinated with food. Food is a part of life—and so it's important to art and to writing. Read the description of the Dutch banquet by Washington Irving. What kind of person would serve a meal like this? Would you like to eat such a meal?

> Such heaped-up platters of cakes of various and almost indescribable kinds, known only to experienced Dutch housewives! There was the doughty doughnut, the tenderer oly koek, and the crisp and crumbling cruller; sweet

cakes and short cakes, ginger-cakes and honey-cakes, and
the whole family of cakes. And then there were apple-pies
and peach-pies and pumpkin pies; besides slices of ham
and smoked beef; and moreover delectable dishes of pre-
served plums, and peaches, and pears, and quinces; not
to mention broiled shad and roasted chickens; together
with bowls of milk and cream, all mingled higgledy-
piggledy, pretty much as I have enumerated them, with
the motherly teapot sending up its clouds of vapor from
the midst. . . .

Now look at this photograph. What does it tell you about the
people eating the meal?

What, where, and how people eat can tell a lot about them—whether they're greedy or picky, rich, middle-class, or poor, friendly or unfriendly, young, old, or middle-aged. What they eat can also suggest the kinds of foods their parents ate, the part of the world or the part of the country they grew up in. You can tell, for example, from Irving's description of the meal that it was served by a wealthy Dutch family, a family that liked to entertain large numbers of people.

Certain foods also seem to go with specific occasions—roast turkey with Thanksgiving, potato latkes with Hanukkah, and baked ham with Easter.

Here's a chance to exercise your imagination. Imagine a room that is bare except for a table and some chairs. Decide who will be eating there and what the occasion will be. Then set the table in your imagination. Choose the tablewear, plates, decorations, and foods that fit the people and occasion you've imagined. For example, if you decide two students will be having an afternoon snack, you might include paper plates, Pepsi, chips, and sandwiches. In setting your imaginary table, you can select items for the following list. You'll also want to add your own choices.

candles in silver candleholders	china plates
centerpiece of dried flowers	cold soup
single rose in a vase	fish sticks
checked tablecloth	pizza
white linen tablecloth	hot-cross buns
plastic place mats	cherries jubilee
paper cups and plates	hot dogs
steak and baked potatoes	pumpkin pie
cottage cheese and mineral water	tacos
small candy mints	frijoles
ceramic coffee mugs	a baked ham
plastic forks, knives, spoons	bologna sandwiches
silver forks, knives, spoons	potato chips
a roast turkey with dressing	fried chicken
peanut-butter sandwiches	Coca-Cola Classic
soft pretzels	meat loaf
chili and soda crackers	fruitcake
collard greens and chitterlings	gefilte fish
raw oysters in a sauce	sukiyaki
champagne in paper cups	Jell-O

liver-dumpling soup	rice pudding
barbecued spareribs	paper hats
silver napkin rings	TV dinner
hominy grits	paper napkins
spaghetti and meatballs	smoked tongue
fried eggplant	Corelle dishes
apple cobbler	pepper mill
corn on the cob	Caesar salad
submarine sandwiches	moussaka
sauerkraut and sausages	candied yams
pancakes and maple syrup	Twinkies
fried onion rings	garlic bread
oatmeal mush	lace tablecloth
homemade cinnamon rolls	sloppy joes
kidneys in wine sauce	lamb curry

After you've set your imaginary table, describe it in words. But first look back at the description of the Dutch banquet by Washington Irving. How does the author make you feel that you're really there, looking at and smelling the foods? Try to write your description so that your reader is there. Also, be sure that your description of the foods helps to illustrate your imaginary characters and the occasion. For example, those two students having a snack probably wouldn't be sitting down to a roast turkey.

3. WRITING POETRY

what a poem is

Spring, love, spring, country streams, spring, and flowers were once the only subjects poetic enough to write poems about. But these days anything goes. Here's a partial list of anything: motorcycles, tennis shoes, hair, what Laura said, drugstore windows, old wooden doors, the smell of leather, red telephones, the word *cool*, dead gardens, park pigeons, rusty iron fences, and, yes, spring.

This is the point: Nothing's poetic, everything's poetic. Poetry isn't something objects, people, places, and feelings have. Poetry is something you put into objects, people, places, and feelings. It's a fresh way of looking. It's seeing the new in the old, the strange in the familiar. Most of all, it's being alive to the world around you.

A poem—to be a poem—doesn't have to have meter or stanzas or rhyme or a title. It can have these things, as you'll see later, but it doesn't have to. A poem doesn't have to be very, very serious, either, or grapple with weighty matters. It can even be funny. In short, there's more than one kind of poetry.

experimental poems

These poems come in all sizes, shapes, and colors. They're really something different. The emphasis is on the visual.

concrete poems

Here's an experimental poem by a student. It's called a concrete poem—only one word and no title.

—Bill Kalal

What a concrete poem does is to act out the meaning of a word. This student, for instance, shaped this word to look like a shark. The *S* forms the tail; the large *A*, the dorsal fin; the *K*, the jaws. And since, as everybody knows, sharks are always hungry, this one is eating a period.

CREATING A CONCRETE POEM

Why not try your own concrete poem? Begin in your journal. Write down some likely words, words that you think could be turned into concrete poems. Here are a few to get you started:

square	explode	ouch
giraffe	smile	rocket
fade	break	shrink

The nice thing about concrete poems is that there are no hard-and-fast rules for making them. You are bound only by the limits of your imagination. Here are a few illustrated tips that may help you:

If you need to repeat a word to make your point, repeat it.

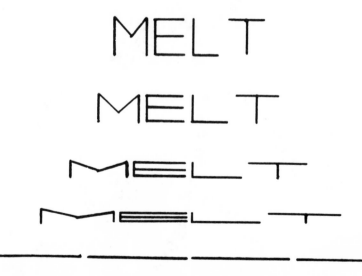

—*Cody J. Trutt*

If you feel like punning, go ahead and pun. The shape of this poem is a pun. It refers to the nickname for the original Volkswagen model, "the bug."

VOLKSWAGEN VOLKSWAGEN
VOLKSWAGEN V W VOLKSWAGEN
VOLKSWAGEN VOLKSWAGEN VOLKS
VOLKSWAGEN VOLKSWAGEN VOLKSWAGE
VOLK SWAG EN VOLKS
VOLK SWAG EN
VOLK SWAG EN
VOLKSWAGEN VOLKSW

—Sue Wilson

Look for phrases as well as single words. Worn-out figures of speech—like "time flies" and "a bolt from the blue"—often make good concrete poems. By visualizing these phrases, you can blow a bit of life into a dead metaphor, as this student has done:

```
bluebluebl        bl            bl          ue        blueblueblu
bl       ue       bl            bl          ue        bl
bl       ue       bl            bl          ue        bl
bl       ue       bl            bl          ue        bl
blueblue          bl            bl          ue        blueblueblu
bl       ue       bl            bl          ue        bl
bl       ue       bl            bl          ue        bl
bl       ue       bl            bl          ue        bl
bluebluebl        bluebluebl    blueblueblu           blueblueblu
```

```
                  boltboltbo
                  boltboltbol
                   boltboltboltb
                    boltboltboltbo
                   oltboltboltbol
                    ltboltboltbolt
                     boltboltboltbolt
                      oltboltboltboltbo
                     ltboltboltboltbol
                  tboltboltboltboltbo
                 ltboltboltboltbolt
               oltboltboltboltbolt
              boltboltboltboltbol
             boltboltboltboltbolt
            boltboltboltboltbolt
            tboltboltboltbolt
             tboltboltboltboltb
              boltboltboltbolt
               boltboltboltbolt
                oltboltboltbol
                 ltboltboltbol
                  tboltbolt
                     bolt
                      olt
```

—*Joyous Masco*

You've seen several ways to make a concrete poem. Now, go ahead and make one of your own. First, look for likely words and phrases. Look in books and newspapers, on billboards and soup cans. You might even thumb through a dictionary. List your finds in your journal. Then let them act out their meaning.

found poems

These poems don't start out as poems. They may start out as copy for advertisements, lists on cereal boxes, shop signs, clauses in insurance policies, forms to be filled out. Only, somewhere along the line, something happened. The words fell together in a special way. They stood out. They added up to a new meaning. What you were reading was no longer just an ad—but a poem!

NEXT TRIP TO ANYWHERE

Famous
carry-on
flight
bag

holds
one
or
two
suits
wrinkle-free
on
a
steel
hanger

just
about
everything
you
need
on
your
next
trip
to
anywhere

Famous
carry-on
flight
bag

just
about
everything
you
need
on
your
next
trip
to
anywhere

You might have to shuffle the words around to make your poem look like a poem. Also, you might want to repeat some of the words and add a title. But, pretty much, you leave things as you found them.

Sometimes, as in the following poems, the words gleaned from a newspaper create new images and appeal to all the senses in unusual ways.

WHY NOT GROW VEGETABLES FOR FUN?

There's a small seed company in Felton, Calif.
It's dedicated to
      seeds not only from France
      but from Holland
And edible flowers
Old fashioned, fragrant flowers
"Scent was considered the soul of flowers"

FISH, LAMB, AND FIGS

Fish, lamb, and figs
like Ancient Greeks
Forget
tomatoes, lemons, and garlic

THE COOKING GARDENER

French haricots
skinny green beans
Swiss chard
so hard to find
leeks
lettuces
chili peppers of course
tomatoes
(a few of my favorites)

—Dan Spinella

DISCOVERING A FOUND POEM

A found poem is a happy accident, like discovering a dollar in the pocket of an old pair of jeans. So look around you. See what you can find on the school bulletin board, in catalogs, in the phone book, in cookbooks. Collect these poems in your journal. If you need a title to make clear what the poem means to you, create one.

paste-pot poems

Here's another kind of experimental poem. Take a look at it and see if you can tell how it was put together.

Part of the fun in making a poem comes from putting together words and ideas that have never been together before—startling words, unusual ideas. As an instance of this, take a look at the poem on the next page. It's experimental, too. But it wasn't just found. Can you tell how it was made? Paste-pot poems, you'll discover, take a little playing around with to get right.

THE INDIAN

WANTS

THE Hunter **WIND** Back

Night *Pottery*

of

Secrets

Birds

Open

the

DANCES

Ripened *Red*

The silent ride

of *the Sun*

63

CREATING A PASTE–POT POEM

The writer of the poem you just read, Norbert Blei, describes how he puts such poems together. He says,

> Take an old newspaper
> Skim through the major and minor headlines, the ads, the women's pages, the comics, the sports section, travel, business, society and obits.

Watch for good words, words like . . .

SQUEEZE

Winter

STRAWBERRIES

Watch for groups of words like "ON CLARK ST., U.S.A.," "ACROSS THE LAND," "IF A CHILD COULD DESIGN A PLAYGROUND," "AH! WHERE ARE THE REBELS OF YESTER-YEAR?"

> Cut these words out
> Mix them freely together
> Arrange them on paper
> Making all kinds of poems
> Then paste them down permanently
> To make your poem stick.

Somewhere in the midst of the making will come the joy.

Somewhere in the midst of joy will come the realization that

...An Artist 'Can Try Anything'

Sounds easy enough, doesn't it? But you'll need lots of words. And you may have to shuffle them around for a while before you produce any interesting combinations. But try it. You'll enjoy pasting together a poem.

alphabet poems

If you like to play Scrabble, you'll probably like to make alphabet poems. Here's one way. Begin your first word with *A*, your second with *B*, and so on, until you come to *Z*. Or go through the alphabet from *Z* to *A*. Here's how one student did it:

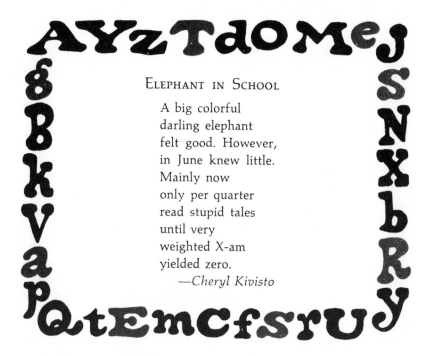

ELEPHANT IN SCHOOL

A big colorful
darling elephant
felt good. However,
in June knew little.
Mainly now
only per quarter
read stupid tales
until very
weighted X-am
yielded zero.
　　　—*Cheryl Kivisto*

You'll have to watch out for *X* and *Z*. Finding words that begin with these letters—and that make some grammatical sense—can be tough. Sometimes you'll have to fake a bit, as this student did for *X*.

You could also write an alphabet poem that spells out its meaning with the first letter of each line, like this:

Buzzing quietly,
Endlessly they
Examine every
Stalk of clover.
　　　—*Jill Robinson*

You'll need to experiment a little. Try several words and phrases. Aim toward a natural-sounding poem.

Try writing both kinds of alphabet poems in your journal. Try to make them grammatical. That's part of the challenge. For the first kind, decide on your general idea and then play around with some of the more difficult words, like those beginning with X, Y, and Z. For the second, jot down five or six words or phrases to start with. Since some will work better than others, only one or two may end up in the finished poem.

free verse

In 1855 Walt Whitman published a book of twelve untitled poems called *Leaves of Grass*. Not too many people liked these poems. People said they were vulgar, dealing with ordinary men and women and familiar places instead of kings and queens and heroes and faraway places. The poems didn't rhyme. What was worse, they didn't have a regular beat, something you could tap your foot to. This was because Walt Whitman wrote in free verse.

He didn't invent free verse. But the more people talked about his poems, the more well-known free verse became. In Whitman's time, free verse was experimental—radical. Not so today.

If free verse doesn't rhyme—and usually it doesn't—and doesn't go ta-DUM, ta-DUM, ta-DUM, then how is it different from prose or from everyday speech? First of all, free verse is more rhythmical than prose. Second, it's more figurative. Third, it has more sensory appeals.

rhythm

The sentences you're reading right now are prose. They have a sort of rhythm. You don't notice it, particularly. And the writer wasn't trying to make you notice it. But when you read free verse, especially out loud, you can hear, almost feel, a lilt or a swing that you don't hear or feel when you read prose. It isn't that prose doesn't have rhythm. It does. But verse, even free verse, has more. Read this poem aloud. Listen for its rhythm.

WORDS ON A WINDY DAY

Airing out the clothes,
   the odor of mothballs
      driving me inside,

I watch in wonder
   as the wind fills
      the trouserlegs and sweaters,

whips them light and dark.
   In that frayed coat
      I courted her a year.

In that old jacket
   married her, then brushed
      her tears off with a sleeve.

The wind blows through them,
   tosses them about,
      these mildewed ghosts of love

that life, for lack of something
   simple as a clothespin,
      let fall, one by one.
         —*Lucien Stryk*

If you listen, you can hear the rhythm, the lilt and the swing, in this poem. Even if these lines had been printed as prose, they would still be more rhythmical than most prose.

But these lines weren't printed as prose. They weren't run together as a four-sentence paragraph. Instead, they were divided into six groups (stanzas, they're called) of three lines each. Why? Because the writer wanted you to notice—to hear—the rhythm of his poem. Dividing the lines as he did, he was trying to make the rhythm visible.

Rhythm is form cut into time.
—Ezra Pound

Suppose you have an idea for a poem. You've begun to work it into lines. Now you think, "How do I divide these lines? Any old way? Or is there some rule I can follow?" Unfortunately, there is no rule. But there are a number of ways that poets divide the lines of free verse. And in the following poem, the writer has used several of them:

Moon Walk

Sure, I know about the *walk*
I think of it
at five in the morning
trucking to the fields.

The moon—
great!
Will my people have to pick fruit there?

I can fill a sack
good
no spaces
till my back hurts
more than my bent Chicano soul.

I'm glad those guys
went to the moon,
let them work
in moon soil
let them journey with crooked backs
in a one-room tube.

Read the second stanza of this student's poem. You'll notice that the first line has two words; the second, only one. The effect of this division is to put heavy emphasis on *the moon* and *great*. These words, then, represent important ideas for the writer. What about the third line? You'll notice that it's a complete sentence— a grammatical unit. So, within a single stanza, the writer has divided her lines in two ways—by emphasis and by grammatical unit.

Now look at the last four lines of this poem. What you find is an independent clause ("let them work") followed by a prepositional phrase ("in moon soil"). Then another independent clause ("let them journey"). What you expect next is another prepositional phrase on the following line. Instead, the prepositional phrase appears on the same line as the clause. Why? You can't be sure. All you can say is that the writer felt this division produced a better rhythm. What do you think? Was she right?

Probably you shouldn't judge line divisions in isolation. Instead, you should read the whole poem and try to get a feel for how the lines work with each other. It's this feel that you need when you divide lines in your own poem. You can't apply rules mechanically. You have to sharpen your ear, to develop a sense of the rhythm of words by playing around with them.

SHOWING RHYTHM

The following poem has been rewritten as prose. Try your hand at dividing the lines. Don't worry about how the lines were originally divided.

> It was an icy day, we buried the cat, then took her
> box and set match to it in the back yard. Those fleas
> that escaped earth and fire died by the cold.
> —*William Carlos Williams*

Williams divided his lines after *day, cat, box, it, yard, escaped,* and *fire.* Did you divide the lines the same places? If not, did his division show the rhythm better? Or do you prefer some of your divisions?

figures of speech

Good verse is a little like concentrated orange juice—the water's been squeezed out. Only the essence is left. Good verse—and that includes good free verse—is somehow thicker, denser, more tightly packed with meaning than most prose.

Mainly, this is because verse makes greater use of figures of speech—especially of metaphor and simile. Read this poem. On a small scale, it shows how metaphor packs extra meaning into the fewest possible words.

TORTOISE

Time-worn
A walking stone
He waits for tomorrow
While pondering the changing world
Watching
—*Ken Lohmann*

A turtle and a stone are basically different. But in this poem they're compared. The writer has called the tortoise "a walking stone." This is a metaphor.

Metaphor   In a metaphor, two things belonging to different classes are linked together. Suppose the writer had called the tortoise a "silvery jet plane." Technically, this is a metaphor. But is it a good one? For a metaphor to work, the things compared must not only be basically different, they must also be alike. A good metaphor is the discovery of similarities between things that are basically different. And when you think about comparing a tortoise to a jet plane, you find only differences.

Go back to the tortoise and the stone. You know they're different, but how are they alike? What about appearance? The gray-black color. And texture? The smoothness and the rough ridges of their surfaces. And shape? The solid, rounded domes.

When you think about it, there are a great many similarities between a tortoise and a stone. This is what makes the metaphor work. An effective metaphor implies a series of similarities without having to list them.

Simile   This figure of speech is like the metaphor, except that the items compared are linked by such words as *like*, *than*, or *as*:

> Like a small grey
> coffee-pot
> sits the squirrel.
> —*Humbert Wolfe*

Though every simile is a comparison, not every comparison is a simile. If you write "Angie sings like Judy Garland," you've written a simple comparison. The items linked by *like* are basically the same. To produce a simile, you have to begin with things that are different. If you write "Angie sings like a bullfrog," then you have a simile.

Basis of comparison   A tortoise does look like a stone. A sitting squirrel does look like a coffeepot. Both figures of speech involve physical comparisons. And they are effective because they are the product of close, accurate observation.

But similes and metaphors do not have to be based on physical resemblance. Here's an effective metaphor that involves no physical comparison:

> My vigor is a new-minted penny;
> Which I cast at your feet.
> —*Amy Lowell*

And here's a famous simile that involves no physical comparison:

> O, my love's like a red, red rose
> —*Robert Burns*

What Lowell and Burns have done is to link the items of their comparisons by emotional associations. Burns isn't saying that his love has a green stem or thorns or roots. Burns wants you to think of the associations of the rose—its beauty and its freshness.

Don't worry too much about the basis of imaginative comparisons. It's enough that you know what your choices are. Nor should you be overly concerned about the distinction between simile and metaphor. What's important for you, as a writer, is that the figures of speech you use are fresh, true, surprising, accurate.

CREATING METAPHORS AND SIMILES

Try writing some metaphors and similes based on the following descriptions:

Umbrellas popping out during a sudden downpour
A friend who bursts angrily into your room
A green Volkswagen with pink and yellow daisies pasted on it
An ambulance speeding through traffic with its siren wailing
A lightning rod on a house
A skyscraper, the top of which is lost in fog
Your boyfriend or girl friend sitting in a chair, saying nothing, dreaming
The sound of someone typing in the next apartment
A thin old woman in a ragged dress
The gruff voice of someone awakened by a wrong telephone number

71

Some of these descriptions may suggest physical comparisons to you. Others, comparisons of emotional associations. The first description, for example, might suggest a simile like this: "Umbrellas, like a patch of mushrooms, sprouted in the rain." For the second description you might write, "Judy was a storm cloud speeding in my direction." Judy doesn't look like a storm cloud. But she has the qualities—energy, destructiveness, speed—usually associated with one.

sensory appeals

Prose tells you about something—that it's cold outside, for instance, or that some people make quiet sacrifices for those they love. Poetry, on the other hand, doesn't settle for the flat, factual statement. Poetry aims at making you live through an experience—cold or love or whatever. And it does this by using sensory appeals.

Words like *idea, relationship, history,* and *spiritual* do not act directly on the senses—at least not in the same way that *salty, velvet, yellow, hissed,* and *musty* do. This second group of words makes you taste, touch, see, hear, and smell. These are the kinds of words a writer uses to make a poem an experience. These are the kinds of words used in this poem:

THOSE WINTER SUNDAYS

Sundays too my father got up early
and put his clothes on in the blueblack cold,
then with cracked hands that ached
from labor in the weekday weather made
banked fires blaze. No one ever thanked him.

I'd wake and hear the cold splintering, breaking.
When the rooms were warm, he'd call,
and slowly I would rise and dress,
fearing the chronic angers of that house,

Speaking indifferently to him,
who had driven out the cold
and polished my good shoes as well.
What did I know, what did I know
of love's austere and lonely offices?

—*Robert Hayden*

72

Words like *blue-black, cold, splintering,* and *breaking* help you to experience the winter morning. Words like *cracked, ached,* and *polished* help you experience the devotion of the father. By using words that appeal directly to your senses, the writer shows you how he felt about his father.

Notice that some of the appeals in this poem act on more than one sense. For instance, the word *cracked* in line 3 has a visual appeal—it shows how the skin of his father's hands looked. But, at the same time, *cracked* appeals to the sense of touch—how the father's hands felt. And, too, there's a suggestion of sound, short and sharp. What about the word *polished* in line 12? Doesn't it also do extra duty?

USING SENSORY APPEALS

Experiment with sensory appeals in your journal. Before each word that follows, add one or more words with sensory appeal. For the first word, you might write *a silver silence, a chill silence, a shattering silence.* This last combination is good because it does double duty by appealing to both sight and sound.

silence	wind
skyscraper	dog
sun	mirror
sky	storm

WRITING FREE VERSE

All along you've been experimenting with aspects of free verse in your journal—with rhythm, figures of speech, sensory images. Now's the time to put them all together and create a poem—or several poems. Go back over what you've written so far. Choose one of your ideas as a start. It could be a figure of speech you'd like to use. Or an unusual rhythm you'd like to try out. Work up your ideas into a poem. And when you finish, ask yourself these questions:

1. Are the lines divided in the best places? Do they help create an interesting rhythm?
2. Are the figures of speech fresh and accurate?
3. Are there enough sensory appeals?

If you can answer "yes" to these questions, then you are on the right track. You may even have written a good poem.

fixed forms

Most people, when they think of poetry, think first of one of the fixed forms—say, a sonnet. Like free verse, the fixed forms of poetry use figures of speech and words that appeal to the senses. Also, like free verse, the fixed forms have rhythm. But here's where the big difference comes in. The rhythm of the fixed forms is far more regular than the rhythm of free verse. That's because the number of syllables, both stressed and unstressed, in each line has already been determined, or fixed.

syllables and stress

Do you know a syllable when you hear one? Say the word *poetry* aloud, slowly. How many syllables do you hear? If you said "three," then you probably understand what a syllable is. You don't need a technical definition. It's enough that you're able to hear syllables.

Now say the word *poetry* again. Which syllable do you put the most force on, say the loudest? If you answered "the first," then you probably understand stress. You understand that the first syllable receives more emphasis than the second and third syllables. For practical purposes, these last two syllables are unstressed.

LISTENING FOR SYLLABLES AND STRESS

Say the following words aloud, slowly. How many syllables does each word have? Which syllable in each word is stressed? Which syllable or syllables are unstressed?

building	forget
book	relentlessly
objective	handy
exam	silently

Here's how it works out. The words are divided into syllables. The stressed syllables are marked with the symbol ´; the unstressed, with the symbol ˘.

buíld ĭng	fŏr gét
boók	rĕ lént lĕss lў
ŏb jéc tĭve	hán dў
ĕx ám	sí lĕnt lў

meter

Read this line aloud. It's from a poem by Robert Frost.

Here come real stars to fill the upper skies

You can hear that some syllables in this line are stressed and some unstressed. You may also have noticed that the stresses occur regularly—on every other syllable, in fact. To describe a pattern like this, you'll need to know a few technical terms. The technical term for the regular rhythm of poetry is *meter*. And the basic unit of meter is the *foot*. A metrical foot consists of one stressed syllable and one or more unstressed syllables. Here's that same line of poetry divided into feet with the syllables marked for stress or the lack of it:

Hĕre cóme | rĕal stárs | tŏ fíll | thĕ úp | pĕr skíes

Notice how the word *upper* is divided in this line. The first syllable is part of one foot; the second, part of another. That's because feet, not words, are the basic units of meter. It's natural to think of words as the basic units of language, but that won't work here. For the moment, forget about words and concentrate only on syllables. These are the building blocks of meter.

A foot with an unstressed syllable followed by a stressed one is called an *iamb*. A line with five feet in it is called *pentameter*. So, by putting the name for the foot and the name for the line together, you get *iambic pentameter*. This is the most commonly used metrical line in English poetry. It's the foundation on which most of the great English poems are built. Here are just a few:

Chaucer's *Canterbury Tales*
Shakespeare's plays
Milton's *Paradise Lost*
Wordsworth's sonnets
Frost's "Death of the Hired Man"

Iambic pentameter is not the only metrical combination in English. If you wrote poetry with six iambs in each line, you would have iambic hexameter; with four iambs, iambic tetrameter. What's more, the iamb isn't the only foot you could use. Here are some other feet:

trochee (hópefŭl): a stressed syllable followed by an unstressed syllable

anapest (ĭn thĕ woóds): two unstressed syllables followed by a stressed syllable

dactyl (prómĭsĭng): a stressed syllable followed by two unstressed syllables

In theory, you could write a poem in trochaic hexameter. Actually, you wouldn't even want to try. Iambic pentameter has worked well for a long time for many writers. This should give you a clue to its usefulness.

When you say that a poem is written in a particular meter, you mean that most of its lines are in that meter. Here's the rest of the poem by Robert Frost. What meter is it in?

FIREFLIES IN THE GARDEN

Hĕre cóme | rĕal stárs | tŏ fíll | thĕ úp | pĕr skiés,
Ănd hére | ŏn eárth | cŏme ém | ŭlá | tĭng fliés
Thăt, thoúgh | thĕy név | ĕr é | quăl stárs | ĭn síze
(Ănd théy | wĕre név | ĕr reál | lў stárs ăt heárt),
Ăchíeve | ăt tímes | ă vér | ў stár- | lĭke stárt.
Ónlў, | ŏf coúrse, | thĕy cán't | sŭstaín | thĕ párt.

You may have noticed something about the meter of the last line. The first foot in this line is a trochee. Why this variation in a line

76

and in a poem that is basically iambic? Partly, because writers can't allow meter to dictate every word they use. After all, a poem has to make sense, too. Partly, also, because some variation in meter helps to avoid monotony. A poem that is totally regular in meter risks sounding singsong.

Meter's measured by the line. So, it might seem natural that when you come to the end of a line, you'd pause. Well, sometimes you do, and sometimes you don't. In the poem you've just read, each of the lines is end-stopped. You pause. The effect is somewhat formal. A more informal, almost conversational effect can be achieved by running your lines on.

> And of course there must be something wrong
> In wanting to silence any song.

A run-on line like this, taken from another poem by Robert Frost, underplays the meter. Which kind of line you use will depend on which effect you're after.

The meter of your poem should match what you're saying. Rhythm and meaning should not work against each other. Here's a stanza of a poem in which that happens. The poem's called "Death" and was written by Percy Bysshe Shelley.

> Death is here, and death is there,
> Death is busy everywhere,
> All around, within, beneath,
> Above is death—and we are death.

For the moment, forget what the words say. Just listen to the rhythm. Doesn't it sound like the kind of meter you'd use to describe a fast game of Ping-Pong? Shelley meant to write a serious, solemn poem. But the fast-paced rhythm undercuts his meaning and makes his poem, unintentionally, a kind of joke. Even great poets goof occasionally. And you can learn from their mistakes. If you're aware that your rhythm must match your meaning, you won't make the kind of mistake Shelley did.

WORKING WITH METER

Even the marking of meter has a technical name. It's called scanning. To see if you've grasped the basics of meter, scan the following poem. Mark the syllables and the feet as you saw them marked for the poem by Robert Frost.

THE SECRET HEART

Across the years he could recall
His father one way best of all.

In the stillest hour of night
The boy awakened to a light.

Half in dreams, he saw his sire
With his great hands full of fire.

The man had struck a match to see
If his son slept peacefully.

He held his palms each side the spark
His love had kindled in the dark.

His two hands were curved apart
In the semblance of a heart.

He wore, it seemed to his small son,
A bare heart on his hidden one,

A heart that gave out such a glow
No son awake could bear to know.

It showed a look upon a face
Too tender for the day to trace.

One instant, it lit all about,
And then the secret heart went out.

But it shone long enough for one
To know that hands held up the sun.
            —Robert P. Tristram Coffin

What would you call the meter of this poem? Are there any variations in it? Where?

rhyme

Probably the most noticeable feature of the fixed forms is rhyme. Words rhyme when they end in syllables that sound alike. The two most common kinds of rhyme in English are masculine and feminine. Masculine rhyme occurs when the "sound-alike" syllables are stressed.

> Jack and *Jill*
>
> Went up the *hill*

If the final syllables are unstressed, then the rhyme is feminine.

> Hey, diddle *diddle*
>
> The cat and the *fiddle*

People like to hear rhyme. It's kind of fun. And in the old days, when poems were memorized, the rhymes were a help in remembering which line came next. But there is more to rhyme than that. A pattern of rhyme can help to hold a poem together. You can use rhyme to bind together the stanzas of your poem. Look at the pattern of rhyme in this poem by Robert Frost. The letters to the right of the poem show which words rhyme with which. The words marked *a*, for example, rhyme, as do the words marked *b*.

ACQUAINTED WITH THE NIGHT

I have been one acquainted with the night.	a
I have walked out in rain—and back in rain.	b
I have outwalked the furthest city light.	a
I have looked down the saddest city lane.	b
I have passed by the watchman on his beat	c
And dropped my eyes, unwilling to explain.	b
I have stood still and stopped the sound of feet	c
When far away an interrupted cry	d
Came over houses from another street,	c
But not to call me back or say good-by;	d
And further still at an unearthly height,	a
One luminary clock against the sky	d
Proclaimed the time was neither wrong nor right.	a
I have been one acquainted with the night.	a

In the first stanza, the word *night* in line 1 rhymes with *light* in line 3. The word *rain* in line 2 rhymes with neither of these but is used as a bridge to the next stanza. And again, in the second stanza, the end word of the middle line, *beat*, serves as a bridge to the third stanza. This "leapfrog" pattern of rhyme is repeated until the last stanza. There you find only two lines, not three. That's because there is no following stanza and no need for a bridge. Notice, also, that the pattern of rhyme has come "full circle." That is, the last line of the poem rhymes with the first line. The writer has used rhyme to frame his poem.

PRACTICING METER AND RHYME

A good way to practice meter and rhyme is to take a well-known poem and write a parody of it, a humorous imitation. You don't even have to start with a very good poem, just one that has a regular rhythm and rhyme. Nor do you have to parody the whole poem. Sometimes just a few lines or stanzas are enough.

Here are two stanzas from Joyce Kilmer's well-known poem "Trees" followed by a parody by Ogden Nash.

> I think that I shall never see
> A poem lovely as a tree.
>
> A tree whose hungry mouth is pressed
> Against the earth's sweet flowing breast.
>
> I think that I shall never see
> A billboard lovely as a tree.
> Indeed, unless the billboards fall
> I'll never see a tree at all.

Now pick a poem and write your own parody.

WRITING FIXED FORMS

Write a poem with regular meter and rhyme. If you like, write a song. That's a poem, too. In fact, you could even steal a tune and write your own words to it. Musicians are always taking somebody's poem and setting it to music. So why not the other way around?

Or you might try writing a haiku. This is a fixed form in which only the number of syllables—not the pattern of stress—is important. A haiku has five syllables in the first line, seven in the second, and five in the third. A haiku is a kind of snapshot in words. Here's one written by a student:

> Ghosts play on children's
> swings, moving them silently
> in the cold moonlight.
> —*Linda Welsh*

You can, if you like, use rhyme in your haiku.

how a poem happens

There's no one way for a poem to come into being. But more often than not, a poem will have its beginning in direct observation. In some unusual incident, perhaps, or some ordinary one that you feel you could build on. Maybe you saw a dog dart across a highway and through heavy traffic. You made a note of it for your journal. Later, you played around with the idea and came up with this:

> This
> fool brave dog
> can he see,
> man's cruel
> machinery?

You've described the scene. You've even produced a rhyme—between *see* and *machinery*. Just because it's free verse doesn't mean you can't use rhyme. But where do you go from here? These lines might jog a memory. You think about your own dog, Rocky, and how he used to chase motorcycles. So you add a few lines about Rocky to the lines you already have.

> Rocky
> your body speeds,
> with man's
> insanity.

So far, so good. But your poem seems incomplete. It lacks a conclusion, a summing up, a punch line. What does this conflict between dogs and machines mean? Maybe you're not sure. Maybe it would be best to put your conclusion in the form of a question.

> Dog,
> what sweet intention
> made you defy
> man's invention?

Now you have a poem. Not a great one, perhaps, but still a poem. It was made of something seen, something remembered, something concluded.

> This
> fool brave dog
> can he see,
> man's cruel
> machinery?
>
> Rocky
> your body speeds,
> with man's
> insanity.
>
> Dog,
> what sweet intention
> made you defy
> man's invention?

MAKING A POEM HAPPEN

This pattern of observation, memory, and conclusion might work for you. First, find a location where there's a lot going on—a busy intersection, a crowded shopping center. Take some notes on what you see. Then, write four lines of free verse about one of the incidents in your notes. After that, search your memory for an experience of your own that relates to this incident. Then, add four more lines. Finally, in four lines, sum up the meaning of the first eight lines. If you wish, the final four lines could be put in the form of a question.

82

in the workshop

Sometimes a poem, usually a short one, will pop into your head whole, complete, and ready to send out into the world. But this is rare. More often than not, you'll have to struggle a little to bring your poem to a finished state. You'll have to cross out words and add new ones, to rearrange lines, add lines, drop lines. You may have to go through three or four versions. You'll do all this so that your readers will respond the way you want them to.

> **Have no fancy ideas about poetry. It doesn't come to you on the wings of the dove. It's something you work hard at.**
>
> **— Louise Bogan**

H. Armstrong Roberts

On the following pages are two versions of an award-winning poem by a student.

The first version is a rough draft. In it the ideas and the words were set down pretty much as they came into the writer's mind. When he was stuck for the right word, he typed a dash and went on. The second version, of course, is a reworking of the first. Here the writer has filled in the missing words and changed others.

With their

white skin

or unremitting cough,

they

doggedly go on

with their daily tasks.

Scarred

from the onslaught

of awful diseases

crippled by

years of

ancient medicine,

they continue to do

what they can.

Unable to pay

for --

they die away

abandoned by everyone,

they simply --

into nothing.

Inheriting much

from their ancestors

they fall into

even more

dreadful ills

passing

these on

to some

descendants

as their legacy.

With their pale skin

or ~~unremitting~~ *their* unremitting cough,

they doggedly

continue
~~go on~~

with their daily tasks.

Scarred

~~from~~ *by* the onslaught

of ~~awful~~ *baffling*

diseases

crippled by years of

medieval ~~ancient~~ medicine,

they continue to do what

they can.

Unable to pay for

the richness of health,

they ~~waste~~ *die* away

abandoned by ~~everyone~~ *all*

they simply fade

into ~~nothing.~~ *oblivion.*

Inheriting much from their

forebears ~~ancestors~~

they ~~fall~~ *plunge*

into

even more

dreadful ills,

passing these on

to some descendants

as

their

legacy.

Examine some of these changes. Why did he change "awful diseases" to "baffling diseases"? Does this change more accurately describe the reaction of the poor? Why was "white skin" changed to "pale skin"? Notice that "die away" was changed to "waste away" and then back to "die away." Which phrase do you prefer?

> **I believe every space and comma is a living part of the poem and has its function, just as every muscle and pore of the body has its function. And the way the lines are broken is a functioning part essential to the life of the poem.**
>
> **—Denise Levertov**

The line divisions of both versions are basically the same. Read the poem as the writer divided the lines. Does the rhythm seem choppy? Here's the final version. Do you think the new line division has improved the rhythm of the poem?

THE IMPOVERISHED

With their pale skin
or their unremitting cough,
they doggedly continue
their daily tasks.
Scarred by the onslaught
of baffling diseases,
crippled by years of
medieval medicine,
they continue to do what they can.
Unable to pay for the privilege of health,
they waste away.
Abandoned by all,
they simply fade into oblivion.
Inheriting much from their forebears,
they plunge
into even more dreadful ills,
passing these on to their descendants
as a legacy.

—Bill Feyerherm

new voices

Nature, war, love, age, youth, joy, death—these are some of the themes of poetry. And they are as old as humanity itself. Yet each generation reacts to these themes in its own voice. Wordsworth and E. E. Cummings have written about spring, but with different voices. Tennyson and Denise Levertov have written about war, but with different voices. Here is a modern voice, speaking about her heritage. Listen!

LEGEND

Sleep, legend, but call me when you wake.
　　　　Your people call, yet hear no answer.

I beg you, legend, heed the call
　　　　Before it is too late.

A tale may die on restless lips, but,
　　　　Legend, wake and say you slept.
　　　　　　　　　　　—Patricia Irving

Patricia Irving is a Native American. Her poem deals with the past and the future. It's about the faith of her people in themselves, which she hopes is not dead, only sleeping. The poem strikes a responsive note. In the past Americans were too ready to give up the past and, as a result, have found themselves rootless. Americans in today's world are finding new strength for the future in the heritage of their past.

Awareness of the past does not always mean "yearning for the good old days." The women's movement is succeeding in expanding roles and opportunities. The following poem expresses one woman's personal frustration with playing the old-fashioned role of meek acceptance. Can a modern woman express her emotions honestly, even anger?

For Witches

today
i lost my temper.

temper, when one talks of metal
means strong,
perfect.

temper, for humans,
means angry
irrational
bad.

today i found my temper.
i said,
you step on my head
for 27 years you step on my head
and though I have been trained
to excuse you for your inevitable
clumsiness
today i think
i prefer my head to your clumsiness.

today i began
to find
myself.

tomorrow
perhaps
i will begin
to find
you.

—Susan Sutheim

It would be hard today to write a poem about the glories of war. The American experience in Vietnam seems to divide generations in their attitude toward war. This poem speaks with a voice of the late '60s.

What Were They Like?

1 Did the people of Viet Nam
  use lanterns of stone?
2 Did they hold ceremonies
  to reverence the opening of buds?
3 Were they inclined to quiet laughter?
4 Did they use bone and ivory,
  jade and silver, for ornament?
5 Had they an epic poem?
6 Did they distinguish between speech and singing?

1 Sir, their light hearts turned to stone.
  It is not remembered whether in gardens
  stone lanterns illumined pleasant ways.
2 Perhaps they gathered once to delight in blossom,
  but after the children were killed
  there were no more buds.
3 Sir, laughter is bitter to the burned mouth.
4 A dream ago, perhaps. Ornament is for joy.
  All the bones were charred.
5 It is not remembered. Remember,
  most were peasants; their life
  was in rice and bamboo.
  When peaceful clouds were reflected in the paddies
  and the water buffalo stepped surely along terraces,
  maybe fathers told their sons old tales.
  When bombs smashed those mirrors
  there was time only to scream.
6 There is an echo yet
  of their speech which was like a song.
  It was reported their singing resembled
  the flight of moths in moonlight.
  Who can say? It is silent now.

—Denise Levertov

Many writers today write about what it's like to be poor. But even in poverty, life can have some very good moments. This poem points out that there are more important things than possessions—like family love.

NIKKI-ROASA

childhood remembrances are always a drag
if you're Black
you always remember things like living in Woodlawn
with no inside toilet
and if you become famous or something
they never talk about how happy you were to have
your mother
all to yourself and
how good the water felt when you got your bath
from one of those
big tubs that folk in chicago barbecue in
and somehow when you talk about home
it never gets across how much you
understood their feelings
as the whole family attended meetings about Hollydale
and even though you remember
your biographers never understand
your father's pain as he sells his stock
and another dream goes
And though you're poor it isn't poverty that
concerns you
and though they fought a lot
it isn't your father's drinking that makes any difference
but only that everybody is together and you
and your sister have happy birthdays and very good
Christmases
and I really hope no white person ever has cause
to write about me
because they never understand
Black love is Black wealth and they'll
probably talk about my hard childhood
and never understand that
all the while I was quite happy

—*Nikki Giovanni*

Speaking of love, today's writer shies away from romantic exag-
geration. You'll find no eyes "like limpid pools," no teeth "like
pearls," no lips "like Cupid's bow" in a poem of today. Instead,
the tone is conversational and the emotion is understated.

Here—Hold My Hand

Here
hold my hand
let me touch you
there is
nothing
we can
say . . . your
soul
eludes me
when I reach
out
your eyes
resent
my need to know
you
here
hold my hand
since
there is nothing
we can
say
—*Mari Evans*

Quill pens and velvet jackets have been out of style for poets for some
time now. These days, a poet is more apt to use a ballpoint and wear
stone-washed jeans. In fact, he may even be an inmate in a prison. And
though this is a special world, it's not so special that an outsider can't
relate to it.

I Say

I say noooooooooooooway
I gonna stay here
forever

nooooooooooooooooway
gonna wait for mail
forever
no way
gonna stay on my knees before the P.A.
praying for names
for visitors
when I know at home
they're living for me
taking my useless life
for a Sunday game.

This chapter began by discussing the wide variety of subject matter and the many different forms poetry can take. Do you remember reading at the beginning of the chapter that a poem doesn't have to be serious? A poem, such as the following one about writing poetry, can be funny and still be good.

Cat!
Get off my
Typewriter! I'm
Off to save the world
With my words. I'll write of
Kings and wars and great
Philosophers. Nothing
Relevant like
Cats.
—*Mark R. Brown*

YOUR OWN VOICE

Do any of the themes you've just read about interest you? Try writing a poem about one of them. You could approach it from a different slant. Or perhaps you don't agree with one of the poems you've read. Then you could write a poem taking the other side. Don't try to write like any other poet. Instead, look for your own voice, your own particular slant on a theme.

4. BASIC FICTION TECHNIQUES

characters

Whatever else a novel or a play is about, it must always be about people. You can't have a story without them. Even those fables you read as a kid were really about people. The clever fox and the vain crow aren't animals at all, but people in disguise. And that goes for Franken-stein's monster and C3P0 and R2D2, too. They're all really people.

Writing about people—that is, creating characters—lies at the heart of all storytelling. People are what other people are most interested in. So the more vivid and lifelike you can make your characters, the more interesting your stories will be.

what they look like

Some ancient philosophers taught that a person's inner self was revealed by his outward appearance. The Latin writer Cicero said, "The face is the image of the soul." Whether true or not, for hundreds of years storytellers have acted on this belief. The good guys have looked good, and the bad guys have looked bad. The handsome Beowulf, for instance, in his gleaming armor, fights Grendel, the monster with the horse's mouth. If you knew nothing else about the characters in this Old English epic, you could tell which was good and which was bad by the way they were described.

The unknown writer of this epic was not the first to use physical descriptions to reveal the inner nature of his characters. Nor was he the last. Here's a modern adventure-story writer describing a villain:

> The face, under the cliff of crew-cut carroty hair, was as startling, without being as ugly, as the body. It was moon-shaped without being moonlike. The forehead was fine and high and the thin sandy brows were level above the large light blue eyes fringed with pale lashes. The nose was fleshily aquiline between high cheek-bones and cheeks that were more muscular than fat. The mouth was thin and dead straight, but beautifully drawn. The chin and jaws were firm and glinted with health. . . .
>
> —*Ian Fleming*

Though not as monstrous as Grendel, Fleming's villain belongs to the same tradition. That is, bad guys who look like bad guys. He has carrot-colored hair, an ugly body, and a thin, straight mouth. His jaws, notes Fleming, "were firm and glinted with health," like those of a well-fed shark.

At this point, you may object. Maybe you remember a mystery story in which the handsome man or the beautiful woman turned out to be the murderer. And what's more, the rumpled, mouse-like detective was the hero, the one who spotted the clue that everyone else missed. But think about this situation for a minute. Is the writer playing fair with you? Isn't the writer simply leading you to expect one thing and then giving you the opposite? It's a trick.

> **The cleverly expressed opposite of any generally accepted idea is worth a fortune to somebody.**
> **—F. Scott Fitzgerald**

Are there only two choices open to the writer of fiction? Create handsome heroes and ugly villains or ugly heroes and handsome villains. Before you answer this, think about another question. Are the people you know completely handsome or completely ugly, completely good or completely bad? Aren't most people a mixture? And if this is so, shouldn't the characters in fiction also be a mixture—especially if a writer is trying to be realistic?

Here's a description of a character taken from a story by Ernest Hemingway. The character, whose name is Wilson, is neither a hero nor a villain. But Hemingway uses details of Wilson's outward appearance to suggest what he is like inside.

> He was about middle height with sandy hair, a stubby mustache, a very red face and extremely cold blue eyes with faint white wrinkles at the corners that grooved merrily when he smiled. He smiled at her now and she looked away from his face at the way his shoulders sloped in the loose tunic he wore with the four big cartridges held in loops where the left breast pocket should have been, at his big brown hands, his old slacks, his very dirty boots and back to his red face again. She noticed where the baked red of his face stopped in a white line that marked the circle left by his Stetson hat that hung now from one of the pegs of the tent pole.

Hemingway writes that Wilson had "extremely cold blue eyes." Wilson is a professional hunter. The cold eyes suggest a detached attitude toward life, a calmness under pressure, and perhaps a reserve in dealing with people. On the other hand, the laugh lines at the corners of his eyes suggest a sense of humor. Wilson, with his red face, is an outdoorsman, but not the kind equipped by expensive sporting-goods stores. The old slacks and dirty boots suggest a casual attitude toward dress.

Hemingway's description may be more realistic than Ian Fleming's and more subtle. But both writers are using the same approach. They are using details of appearance to reveal what their characters are really like. They are not offering you photographs in words. Many details have been excluded from their descriptions. Only those that reveal the characters' emotional makeup are used.

DESCRIBING APPEARANCE

The wanted poster hanging on the police-station wall serves a specific purpose: to identify someone sought for a crime. Usually, there's a photograph plus some descriptive details—name, sex, color of hair and eyes, age, weight, height.

Try this in your journal. Describe a friend or a relative as though you were writing a wanted poster. Your description might read like this:

> Tom Holman is seventeen years old. He is 5 feet 10 inches tall and weighs 155 pounds. He has dark brown eyes and thick, curly black hair. There is a small mole under his left eye.

This kind of description might help someone pick Tom Holman out of a lineup, but it doesn't tell you what Tom is like. It doesn't tell you whether Tom is friendly or cold, generous or mean, shy or pushy. It doesn't tell you whether he is self-conscious or casual, funny or dull. And these are the emotional traits that a fiction writer wants to reveal. These are the kinds of traits that a writer uses physical details to suggest.

So enlarge upon your basic description. Use physical details to show what the person is really like. Suppose Tom Holman is the friendly, outgoing type. Then you might write, "Tom's wide-open laugh came from deep down, from his toes, and made even passersby who heard it smile." Suppose Tom Holman is a very serious sort of person. You might write, "His eyes were almost black, like two holes burned in a piece of paper." Suppose he is carefully casual. You might write, "Faded jeans were a uniform for Tom. And, of course, the battered sneakers with the bright green laces." Suppose he is the nervous type. You might write, "Tom kept playing with his class ring, slipping it on and off his finger as he talked." These are only a few of the ways you could use physical details to show what a person is like. Remember, your purpose is to reveal the inner person, not to list photographically every detail of physical appearance.

how they act

Why not just write that so-and-so is stingy or generous, funny or dull—and be done with it? Wouldn't this be the best way to tell your readers what a character is like? Clearly, it's the most direct way.

Labeling people with adjectives is direct, but kind of dull. It's probably dull because it's not lifelike. In life you don't know, for example, that someone's stingy. You find out that he's stingy. You see him being stingy. Then you make your judgment. This is how it works in fiction, too. The writer shows you someone being stingy and lets you form a judgment.

> **In writing stories of any length, the most important thing to keep in mind is "show, don't tell."**
>
> **—Ben Bova**

Suppose you are going to write a play. And your main character is going to be someone who is selfish and cruel. How would you go about showing these traits to your audience? Here's how one dramatist did it. First, he created a minor character whose traits contrasted with those of the major character. Miss Tesman is kind, simple, and modest. The dramatist, Henrik Ibsen, then has Miss Tesman pay a visit to her nephew George and his new wife Hedda. In the first scene, the audience learns what kind of person Miss Tesman is.

> TESMAN: (*With the bonnet in his hand, looks at it from all sides.*) Why, what a gorgeous bonnet you've been investing in!
> MISS TESMAN: I bought it on Hedda's account.
> TESMAN: On Hedda's account? Eh?
> MISS TESMAN: Yes, so that Hedda needn't be ashamed of me if we happened to go out together.
> TESMAN: (*Patting her cheek.*) You always think of everything, Aunt Julia. (*Lays the bonnet on a chair beside the table.*) And now, look here—suppose we sit comfortably on the sofa and have a little chat, till Hedda comes. (*They seat themselves. She places her parasol in the corner of the sofa.*)

Then Hedda enters. She is the main character, the one who's cruel and selfish. And it is her personality that Ibsen is most interested in revealing. Hedda knows that the bonnet on the chair belongs to Miss Tesman.

> HEDDA: (*Interrupting.*) We shall never get on with this servant, Tesman.

101

MISS TESMAN: Not get on with Berta?

TESMAN: Why, dear, what puts that in your head? Eh?

HEDDA: (*Pointing.*) Look there! She has left her old bonnet lying about on a chair.

TESMAN: Why, Hedda—

HEDDA: Just fancy, if anyone should come in and see it.

TESMAN: But Hedda—that's Aunt Julia's bonnet.

HEDDA: Is it!

MISS TESMAN: (*Taking up the bonnet.*) Yes, indeed it's mine. And, what's more, it's not old, Madam Hedda.

HEDDA: I really did not look closely at it, Miss Tesman.

MISS TESMAN: (*Trying on the bonnet.*) Let me tell you, it's the first time I have worn it—the very first time.

TESMAN: And a very nice bonnet it is, too—quite a beauty!

MISS TESMAN: Oh, it's no such great thing, George. (*Looks around her.*) My parasol—? Ah, here. (*Takes it.*) For this is mine, too—(*mutters*)—not Berta's.

TESMAN: A new bonnet and a new parasol! Only think, Hedda!

HEDDA: Very handsome indeed.

TESMAN: Yes, isn't it? Eh? But Auntie, take a good look at Hedda before you go! See how handsome she is!

MISS TESMAN: Oh, my dear boy, there's nothing new in that. Hedda was always lovely.

Brut Productions

What kind of person would go out of her way to insult her new husband's aunt? Would care more about a tidy room than about the feelings of others? Ibsen shows you Hedda in action, and the kind of person she is comes through strong and clear. This is much more effective than having someone say, "That Hedda, she has a mean streak in her."

Showing, instead of telling, is important for all fiction—not just for drama. Even in a brief short story, the characters will seem more interesting and more lifelike if you have them act out their personality and leave it up to your readers to judge what kinds of people they are.

SHOWING YOUR CHARACTERS IN ACTION

Look at the following statements. Each describes a person with a particular trait. Convert these statements into actions that show what the persons are like.

1. Carlos has trouble making up his mind.
2. Anita is stingy.
3. Doris can get mad all of a sudden.
4. Cindy is aggressive.
5. Maria is a shy person.
6. Mr. Chang is witty.
7. Mr. Potter is nervous.
8. Judy doesn't like to study.
9. Brian is carefree.
10. Becky loves people.

For the first statement, you might write something like this:

> Each morning Carlos sat on the edge of his bed debating whether to put on his right sock first or his left one.

You may, if you wish, use dialogue. For example, the second statement might be handled this way:

> MARY: Did you buy a transfer?
> ANITA: No. I've got yesterday's. Why pay when I can get a free ride?

what's important to them

How do you feel about war? And how do you feel about money, religion, the future, love, work? You probably have strong, deep feelings about these things. And if you said what you felt about any one of them, truly and fully, you would reveal a great deal about yourself. By the same token, if you created a character for a story and had him express his feelings about injustice, say, or politics, you would be giving your readers an insight into his personality. The problem for you, as a writer, is doing this in a way that seems natural.

People don't ordinarily go around delivering speeches on weighty matters. They are far more likely to chat about the weather. Only when they are angered or shocked or saddened, when they are under some emotional pressure, do they release their deepest feelings. And in doing so, they reveal a lot about themselves. Similarly, in a play or a story, if a character expresses deep feelings about life, he must do so for a reason. Something must move him to reveal himself in this way.

Here's a scene from the play *Raisin in the Sun* by Lorraine Hansberry. In it, the character Mama expresses her feelings about love and forgiveness. But Lorraine Hansberry has prepared her audience for this speech. Mama is defending her son Walter. He has just squandered the family's life savings on a get-rich-quick scheme. Mama's daughter, Beneatha, is bitter about what her brother has done. It was her money, too, that Walter lost. She says to Mama,

BENEATHA: Love him? There is nothing left to love.
MAMA: There is always something left to love. And if you ain't learned that, you ain't learned nothing. (*Looking at her.*) Have you cried for that boy today? I don't mean for yourself and for the family 'cause we lost the money. I mean for him; what he been through and what it done to him. Child, when do you think is the time to love somebody the most; when they done good and made things easy for everybody? Well then, you ain't through learning—because that ain't the time at all. It's when he's at his lowest and can't believe in hisself 'cause the world done whipped him so. When you starts measuring somebody, measure

him right, child, measure him right. Make sure you done taken into account what hills and valleys he come through before he got to wherever he is.

What did you learn about the character Mama from this speech? Can you describe her values? Which is more important to her—people or money? Is she the kind of person who holds a grudge? The speech is not long. But the writer has packed several important insights into it. And it's effective because the writer has given the character a reason for saying what she does.

REVEALING BASIC ATTITUDES

Here are some situations that might prompt a person to express strong feelings and reveal a basic attitude. Study them and be prepared to write a paragraph or two in which the character expresses his or her feelings.

1. Fred has just been told by the manager of the store in which he works that he is not paying enough attention to the customers.
2. Wilma is stopped on the street by a beggar who asks her for money for a meal.
3. Carolyn is called to the principal's office and told that her younger brother has been killed in an automobile accident.
4. Virginia finds an envelope with $1500 in it on the floor of the bus.
5. Jon has just been stopped by a traffic officer for running a red light.
6. Steve meets his girl Dolores coming out of a movie theater with his best friend Terry.
7. Marcia has just won a college scholarship.
8. Becky has learned her parents are getting a divorce.

Suppose you decided to use the first situation. Your purpose is to reveal how the character Fred feels about his job in particular and work in general. You might have Fred say the following to another employee:

> Am I ticked off! Every time I start reading my paperback, some dumb customer comes along and wants something. If it's not a salt-and-pepper set, it's an electric can opener or triple-0 steel wool. And imagine that Mrs. Gonzales! Imagine her saying I was goofing off. What kind of manager is she, anyway? With all these customers in here today, I'm never going to finish this book.

If none of the situations listed here appeal to you, invent your own or pick one from your journal. Then create a character. Or two characters, if you need them. You might, for example, create two characters talking about the same kind of job, but from contrasting points of view. Remember, what they say should reveal how they feel—about their job or people or life or all of these.

what they're called

Finding the right names for your characters isn't the most important part of writing fiction. But it's not insignificant, either. Some writers make up colorful names that exaggerate a character's traits. In the novels of Charles Dickens, for instance, there's Serjeant Buzfuz, a tricky lawyer, and Mr. Bumble, a minor official puffed up with a sense of his own importance. There are the pious frauds Pecksniff and Uriah Heep and the all-time miser, Ebenezer Scrooge.

Other writers prefer realistic names. The French novelist Georges Simenon, for instance, keeps telephone directories from all over the world. If one of his characters is from Rome, he will go through the phone book of that city until he finds just the right name. He feels that a made-up name never sounds as real as a real name.

Which method you use in naming your characters will depend on the kind of story you're writing. Colorful names might work well in a humorous story, but be out of place in a realistic one. And for a science-fiction story, you might need special names like Zorg-1 or Fiz-2. Here's the point: Professional writers are careful in selecting names for their characters. You should be, too.

NAMING CHARACTERS

Invent names for the following characters. Write them down and bring them to class. Compare your names with those selected by other members of the class.

1. A sheriff of a small midwestern town
2. A chief of police of a large eastern city
3. A check-out clerk in a supermarket
4. A Hollywood starlet
5. A country-and-western singer
6. A private detective
7. A bullfighter
8. A foreign correspondent
9. A shopkeeper in a small New England town
10. A writer of mystery stories

As a switch, you might like to try this. Invent a name and see whether the other members of your class can guess the type of character you had in mind.

setting

Fiction has to have settings. It has to have descriptions of the places where and when the events happen. The question is, how much space, how many words, should be given over to describing setting?

> **Your descriptions are often more minute than will be liked. You give too many particulars.**
>
> **—Jane Austen**

In the classic French theater the rule was that you never put a chair on stage unless someone was going to sit on it. The set was kept simple and uncluttered. If something wasn't going to be used, it didn't belong. That's not a bad rule to bear in mind—and act on. Applied to describing setting, it would mean limiting yourself to a few vivid details. And in a very short story, you might use only a couple of sentences. So the thing to do is to move in close, to describe your setting as though you were standing a few yards away, like this:

> The rain stopped as Nick turned into the road that went up through the orchard. The fruit had been picked and the fall wind blew through the bare trees. Nick stopped and picked up a Wagner apple from beside the road, shiny in the brown grass from the rain. He put the apple in the pocket of his Mackinaw coat.   —*Ernest Hemingway*

And like this:

> It was mid-morning—a very cold, bright day. Holding a potted plant before her, a girl of fourteen jumped off the bus in front of the Old Ladies' Home, on the outskirts of town. She wore a red coat, and her straight yellow hair was hanging down loose from the pointed white cap all the little girls were wearing that year. She stopped for a moment beside one of the prickly dark shrubs with which the city had beautified the Home, and then proceeded slowly toward the building, which was of white-washed brick and reflected the winter sunlight like a block of ice....   —*Eudora Welty*

It's usual to open a story with a description of setting. But you don't have to. Here, in fact, is a short story that begins with dialogue. The setting, a beauty parlor, is described briefly but vividly between the lines of dialogue.

> "Reach in my purse and git me a cigarette without no powder in it if you kin, Mrs. Fletcher, honey," said Leota to her ten o'clock shampoo-and-set customer. "I don't like no perfumed cigarettes."
>
> Mrs. Fletcher gladly reached over to the lavender shelf under the lavender-framed mirror, shook a hair net loose from the clasp of the patent-leather bag, and slapped her hand down quickly on a powder puff which burst out when the purse was opened.
>
> "Why, look at the peanuts, Leota!" said Mrs. Fletcher in her marveling voice. —*Eudora Welty*

Right away, you know where you are in this story. The writer hasn't wasted words putting you in the picture.

How many words you spend describing setting will depend partly on how long your story runs. For a longer story—for a novel, say—you might move away from your setting. You might begin by giving your readers a bird's-eye view like this:

> The village of Holcomb stands on the high wheat plains of western Kansas, a lonesome area that other Kansans call "out there." Some seventy miles east of the Colorado border, the countryside, with its hard blue skies and desert-clear air, has an atmosphere that is rather more Far West than Middle West. The local accent is barbed with a prairie twang, a ranch-hand nasalness, and the men, many of them, wear narrow frontier trousers, Stetsons, and high-heeled boots with pointed toes. The land is flat, and the views are awesomely extensive; horses, herds of cattle, a white cluster of grain elevators rising as gracefully as Greek temples are visible long before a traveler reaches them. —*Truman Capote*

Remember, if you describe the setting from this far away, you'll need several paragraphs, maybe more, to move up to your characters and the action of the story. A description like this may be very effective at the beginning of a novel. But if you put it at the beginning of a short story, you'll throw the story badly off balance, make it top-heavy. For a short story, you must stay closer to the setting.

> **But in general, for the purposes of most novelists, the number of objects genuinely necessary for . . . [describing a scene] will be found to be very small.**
>
> **—Elizabeth Bowen**

Whatever the length of the story you're writing, don't tell your readers more than they need to know. It's easy, especially for a young writer, to get carried away with descriptions. But for most readers, setting is probably the least interesting part of fiction. Keep your readers in mind as you write and as you revise what you've written. And think of setting as background, as so much scenery for your characters to perform in front of. Avoid piling up details. If you spend too many words on setting, the background will overpower your characters and their actions and, what's worse, bore your readers.

CREATING A SETTING

Setting is not an end in itself. It's only part of a story, and in modern short fiction, not the most important part. Read the following character descriptions. Imagine the setting in which each of these characters would appear. Then write a paragraph or two describing one of these characters and the setting. Assume that you are writing a short story and view the setting from close up.

1. A professor of philosophy who has taken a summer job driving a city cab
2. A homemaker, the mother of three, who lives in a humdrum suburb but daydreams of visiting far-off, exciting places
3. A hired killer waiting for his prey
4. An elderly clergyman walking along a crowded beach on a Sunday afternoon
5. A young man, a former member of a traveling rock band, who decides to take a nine-to-five office job

6. A newly graduated policewoman who is on her first night on the job

You might find it effective to describe setting through the eyes of your character. Suppose, for example, that you have chosen to describe the professor driving a cab. Then you might write something like this:

> Logic was no help at all in driving crosstown during the rush hour. Up ahead Rogan could see a solid jam of buses. No taxis. Experienced taxi drivers avoided Forty-sixth Street. The buses had no choice.
>
> The rubber on the wipers was dead and only smeared his windshield. But Rogan could see that the pedestrians hurrying along the sidewalks under their glistening umbrellas were making better time than he was.

narrative focus

Suppose you have an idea for a short story. You mull it over, think about your characters and what happens to them. You take some notes in your journal. Then, just to get things straight in your mind, you write a fairly detailed outline of the plot.

> Ever since he left school, Alfred Higgins has had a hard time holding a job. Something always happens. But six months ago, he found a job as a clerk in a small drugstore. During that time, Alfred has taken small items from the store and sold them for extra money. One night at closing, Alfred's employer, Sam Carr, confronts Alfred and forces him to admit that he has been stealing. Sam Carr threatens to have Alfred arrested. He calls Alfred's home and talks to his mother, who hurries down to the store. Mrs. Higgins arrives and calmly persuades Sam Carr not to prosecute her son. She and Alfred return home together. Later, Alfred decides to compliment his mother on her handling of Sam Carr. He goes to the kitchen where she is making tea. He observes her without her seeing him. He is struck by the change in her manner. Instead of the smiling, confident woman in the drugstore, he sees now a trembling, discouraged, defeated woman.

Now comes the big question. How do you convert a journal entry like this into a short story? In other words, how do you put flesh on the skeleton and make it breathe and live?

First, even before you begin to write, think some more about a starting place. Should you begin your story with Alfred's first day on the job? If you do, what happens? For one thing, you'll have to describe the whole period leading up to Sam Carr's confronting Alfred. You'll probably have to show Alfred being tempted to steal, giving in to the temptation, and then selling the items he steals. If you start with Alfred's first day on the job, you may find yourself with too much material, more material than you can easily fit into a short story.

So what choice do you have? You could begin in the middle. There's no rule that says you have to begin a story at the point in time that sets the action in motion. So why not start with Sam Carr accusing Alfred of being a thief? And mention in passing that Alfred has worked in the store for six months. This way you'll be starting your story close to the conflict, close to a situation that will grab the attention of your readers.

All right. You know where to begin. But how do you tell your story? What choices do you have in presenting your material? If you look closely at some well-written stories, you'll discover that writers have three basic methods of presenting their material —scene, summary, and description. To take the last of these first, description is used to tell something about characters and settings by showing what they look like. You've already read several examples of description. And you've learned that modern writers tend to play down description. Large chunks of description, particularly in a short story, tend to clog the flow of the narrative.

Writers use summary to bridge gaps, to move rapidly over several events, to condense information that's important to the story but not important enough to show in detail. Summary gives a general account of what happened. If you started the story of Alfred Higgins with a summary, it might read like this:

> Just after closing time in the drugstore, Alfred Higgins was stopped by his employer, Sam Carr, who said that Alfred had been stealing from the store for the last six months. Alfred denied at first that he had taken anything . . .

Beginning this story as a summary would be a mistake. The situation of Alfred's getting caught is attention-grabbing and important. After all, that's why you're beginning the story here and not with Alfred's first day on the job. The way to present this material is in a scene. That's how the writer of the story, Morley Callaghan, did it.

> They were closing the drugstore, and Alfred Higgins, who had just taken off his white jacket, was putting on his coat and getting ready to go home. The little gray-haired man, Sam Carr, who owned the drugstore, was bending down behind the cash register, and when Alfred Higgins passed him, he looked up and said softly, "Just a moment, Alfred. One moment before you go."
>
> The soft, confident, quiet way in which Sam Carr spoke made Alfred start to button his coat nervously. He felt sure his face was white. Sam Carr usually said, "Good night," brusquely, without looking up. In the six months he had been working in the drugstore Alfred had never heard his employer speak softly like that. His heart began to beat so loud it was hard for him to get his breath.

"What is it, Mr. Carr?" he asked.

"Maybe you'd be good enough to take a few things out of your pocket and leave them here before you go," Sam Carr said.

"What things? What are you talking about?"

"You've got a compact and a lipstick and at least two tubes of toothpaste in your pocket, Alfred."

"What do you mean? Do you think I'm crazy?" Alfred blustered. His face got red and he knew he looked fierce with indignation. But Sam Carr, standing by the door with his blue eyes shining bright behind his glasses and his lips moving underneath his gray mustache, only nodded his head a few times, and then Alfred grew very frightened and he didn't know what to say. Slowly he raised his hand and dipped it into his pocket, and with his eyes never meeting Sam Carr's eyes, he took out a blue compact and two tubes of toothpaste and a lipstick, and he laid them one by one on the counter.

"Petty thieving, eh, Alfred?" Sam Carr said. "And maybe you'd be good enough to tell me how long this has been going on."

"This is the first time I ever took anything."

"So now you think you'll tell me a lie, eh? What kind of a sap do I look like, huh? I don't know what goes on in my own store, eh? I tell you you've been doing this pretty steady," Sam Carr said as he went over and stood behind the cash register.

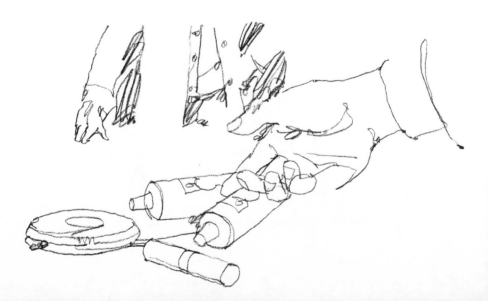

A scene in a short story—and in a novel, too—is handled in much the same way as a scene in a play. The writer focuses on a specific action at a specific time in a specific place. And usually, he uses dialogue, as Callaghan did here.

The scene gives a reader the sense of watching something happen —now. Summary, on the other hand, is useful in relating past events. Here is Callaghan using summary in the next paragraph:

> Ever since Alfred had left school he had been getting into trouble wherever he worked. He lived at home with his mother and his father, who was a printer. His two older brothers were married and his sister had got married last year, and it would have been all right for his parents now if Alfred had only been able to keep a job.

Description is often used to introduce a scene. Here Callaghan describes Mrs. Higgins as she enters the drugstore. She is the only character in this story who is described fully.

> Mrs. Higgins must have been going to bed when he telephoned, for her hair was tucked in loosely under her hat, and her hand at her throat held her light coat tightly across her chest so her dress would not show. She came in, large and plump, with a little smile on her friendly face. Most of the store lights had been turned out and at first she did not see Alfred, who was standing in the shadow at the end of the counter. Yet as soon as she saw him she did not look as Alfred thought she would look: she smiled, her blue eyes never wavered, and with a calmness and dignity that made them forget that her clothes seemed to have been thrown on her, she put out her hand to Mr. Carr and said politely, "I'm Mrs. Higgins. I'm Alfred's mother."

This description of the calm, confident Mrs. Higgins contrasts with the description of her given near the end of the story.

> Leaning back in the chair, she sighed and lifted the cup to her lips, and her lips were groping loosely as if they would never reach the cup. She swallowed the hot tea eagerly, and then she straightened up in relief, though her hand holding the cup still trembled. She looked very old.

115

Now notice how Callaghan moves smoothly from one narrative focus to another, from description to summary.

It seemed to Alfred that this was the way it had been every time he had been in trouble before, that this trembling had really been in her as she hurried out half-dressed to the drugstore. He understood why she had sat alone in the kitchen the night his young sister had kept repeating doggedly that she was getting married. Now he felt all that his mother had been thinking of as they walked along the street together a little while ago. He watched his mother, and he never spoke, but at that moment his youth seemed to be over; he knew all the years of her life by the way her hand trembled as she raised the cup to her lips. It seemed to him that this was the first time he had ever looked upon his mother.

When you write, think of your story as having rhythm, a movement. When you stop the rhythm, telling your readers what you see or what one of your characters sees, you are describing. When you slow the rhythm, detailing specific action, thoughts, and words, you are producing a scene. When you speed up the rhythm, giving a general account of thoughts and actions, you are summarizing.

> **Good writers will, indeed, do well to imitate the ingenious traveller . . . who always proportions his stay in any place.**
>
> **—Henry Fielding**

Clearly, the scene is reserved for important moments, moments of crisis and high tension. The summary is useful for filling in background, building transitions from one scene to another, and explaining the meaning of events. Description can be used to introduce scenes and to record change, to show the effects of events upon the characters and the settings.

BUILDING A SCENE

Here are some basic story situations, just as they might appear in your journal. Read them over. Use one of them to build a scene for a short story. If you can, extend your writing to include description and summary. If none of these situations appeal to you, use a situation from your journal.

Ann is talking with her friend Sonja in a hamburger joint late one afternoon. Ann is worried about an upcoming math test. Her grades have to improve, or she won't get into college. Sonja offers to show Ann a surefire way to cheat on the test. Ann knows she shouldn't cheat. She even likes her teacher, Mrs. Sheridan. But she's really on the spot about her grades. She thinks it wouldn't do any harm to listen to Sonja.

Dan Mathers meets Juanita Gomez coming out of the dry cleaner's on Saturday afternoon. Dan and Juanita used to go together, but broke up about three weeks ago. Dan misses Juanita, hopes she misses him, and wonders whether he should just ask her for a date.

Carla is baby-sitting with the Norton twins. She's just put them to bed upstairs when she hears a noise downstairs, as though somebody were trying to break into the house.

Darlene and her mother are spending an evening at home watching television. During a break for commercials, Mrs. Turl announces that she is going to get married again. Darlene is surprised. She doesn't like the man her mother's going to marry. She doesn't want anyone to take her father's place. She tries to change her mother's mind.

symbols

Washing your hands is a pretty ordinary thing to do. If the action means anything, it means only that your hands are dirty. But when Shakespeare has the sleepwalking Lady Macbeth try to wash the imagined blood from her hands, this simple act takes on a larger meaning. It symbolizes Lady Macbeth's attempt to rid herself of guilt for what she has done.

Writers often use ordinary acts and even objects in this special way, to connect with a larger, more universal meaning. A stopped clock, for instance, in a short story may signal the death of one of the characters. A bird with broken wings may represent the failed hopes of the hero. The bird and the clock have become symbols. They stand for more than themselves.

Here's part of a short story that uses a symbol very effectively. See if you can tell what it is and what it means. The story was written by a high-school student. It's about a boy named Joe and his older sister Delly. They are poor. One hot summer day they take a bus to the public swimming pool. But the man in charge won't let them in.

> I never saw the man's eyes. Just his mouth. He had a gold tooth in front and I remembered it wasn't pretty like most gold but kinda dull and brassy looking. That gold tooth just seemed to glare at me and I knew that he was saying "no" cause we had no place in his pool or any

pool where people had gold in their mouth. Delly and me, we didn't have gold anyplace. Not even that cheap gold paint they have on dishes or on those fake statues you win at carnivals. So I followed Delly to the bus stop and we just sat there. She was crying, but I didn't know why, cause she should have known better than to try and get in some place where people were rich with gold. We got on the bus finally and it jerked sudden, like it always does. And my dry, neatly folded swim suit fell off my lap and on to the floor next to an old woman who kicked it back over to me. When we got home and told Mother why we didn't get to swim, she said we had to expect that cause we were poor and didn't have any gold and a lot of people didn't understand.

In this excerpt gold is more than just a piece of dental work. It's also a symbol. It's used to represent money and power. It stands for a hard, unyielding attitude. It separates those who can use the pool from those who cannot. It is effective as a symbol because it includes all these meanings but remains a real object in the story, a tooth in a person's mouth. That's where the skill comes in: being able to deepen and enlarge the meaning of a story with symbols that fit in naturally and easily.

How do you do this? You could write a first draft of your story and then go back and sprinkle it with symbols. But that won't work. In fact, if you try it, you may spoil an otherwise good story. Instead, when you're writing your first draft, don't think about symbols at all. Then, as you read over what you've written, look for some object or situation that seems to have a special meaning. As you revise, try to sharpen this meaning. Make the symbol clear to your readers. After all, a symbol that has meaning only for you isn't much of a symbol. If you don't discover a symbolic situation or object as you revise, then forget it. There are plenty of vivid, interesting stories and plays that have no symbols in them.

5. WRITING A ONE-ACT PLAY

begin with a situation

So you want to write a play. Or at least you think you do. But first, you want to know what you're letting yourself in for. For example, where do you start?

You start with a situation—the story of an event, a happening. Not necessarily a full-blown, detailed story. It could be just an anecdote you heard. Or perhaps an incident you found interesting enough to write down in your journal.

But why not start with a character? Why not take a person who leads an exciting life—a newspaper reporter, a spy, a business tycoon—and then invent situations for this character? After all, many novelists and short-story writers work this way.

You could begin with a character. But if you do, there's a danger that your play may center around the character's inner thoughts and feelings. That's fine for a short story. But not for a play. In a play, there's really no good way to show what's going on in a character's mind, not without shattering the illusion of reality. It would be a mistake, for example, to try to write a play about someone who sits silently in a room and broods. On the other hand, you might find it easy to write a short story about such a character.

The point here is simple. If you start with a situation, rather than a character, you'll stand a better chance of developing material that can be presented on a stage.

> **When I construct a play I think first in terms of a story.**
>
> **—John Arden**

All right. You're going to begin with a situation. But what kind of situation? What kind of story is most likely to make an interesting play?

First of all, it must be a situation that centers on a conflict, a struggle, a problem. If you like, think in terms of sports, one team pitted against another. That's pure conflict.

Secondly, the outcome of the conflict must not be obvious in advance. There must be some suspense. A lopsided game, for instance, won't hold the fans' attention as well as one in which the teams are well matched.

122

Finally, the conflict must be significant. Something important must be at stake. You won't get far showing a character torn between mushrooms and anchovies for his pizza. True, there is conflict in the situation. But a conflict like this isn't weighty enough to interest an audience. Whether the character finally chooses mushrooms or anchovies doesn't make much difference.

The curious thing is that a conflict of some significance is needed even for comedy. In a famous comedy, *The Importance of Being Ernest,* a young man needs to learn who his parents are in order to marry the girl he loves. You can't tell from this statement that *The Importance of Being Ernest* is a comedy. Usually, the difference between comedy and tragedy, between funny plays and sad ones, is not in the kind of conflict involved. It's in the way the writer looks at the conflict.

These, then, are three basic things you should look for in developing a situation for a one-act play—or for any other type of drama. The situation must have conflict and suspense, and it should be about something important. What else should you look for?

Assume that the play you're going to write is a short one. You're not planning, for instance, a five-act verse tragedy about Joan of Arc. For a short play, you should look for a situation involving only a few characters—say, two or three. Look for a situation that takes place in a brief span of time—maybe just a few hours at the most. Finally, look for a situation that involves no more than one change, or at the most two changes, of scene.

And don't worry because you can't show your characters' inner thoughts and feelings. By focusing on the conflict, your audience will become emotionally involved in the fate of your characters. The conflict will make your characters seem like real people.

LOOKING FOR DRAMATIC POTENTIAL

Read each of the following situations. Which ones have dramatic potential? Why? Be prepared to discuss them in class. Can you change any of the situations that lack dramatic potential into good material for drama? Which ones? How?

1. Dave's father discovers a duplicate key that Dave has had made for the family car.

2. Sylvia can't decide whether to go to class or meet her boyfriend at the Snack Shop.

3. Margo wants to run for a seat in the House of Representatives, but if she is elected, it would mean spending considerable time away from her husband.

4. Annette's friend Melva gives her a copy of an upcoming math test.

5. Sharon is entertaining dinner guests whom she wants to impress. When she goes into the kitchen to get her lobster Newburg, which she had just placed on the counter, she discovers that the cat has started eating it. She is dismayed, but she puts the cat outside and sprinkles a little cheese on top of the casserole and sticks it under the broiler for a minute. She then serves the dish. About halfway through the dinner she notices through the dining room window that the cat seems to be having convulsions out in the driveway.

6. An hour before her wedding, Linda receives a phone call from her fiancé Paul, who says he wants to back out.

7. Janet's mother has always regretted that she didn't get to go to college. She wants Janet to go, but Janet doesn't feel she is college material.

8. Jim has just won $10,000 in the lottery and can't decide how to spend it.

9. Phil's friend Richard, who works as a cashier in the school cafeteria, frequently helps himself to money from the till. Phil thinks this is wrong, but he hesitates to turn his friend in.

10. Tom's seventy-year-old mother has had a stroke and is no longer able to live alone. Tom wants her to come and live with him and his wife Clarice, but Clarice feels it would be better for the mother to live in a home with other elderly people.

CHOOSING A SITUATION

Pick one of the previous situations that you think you could turn into a brief play. If you like, select one from your journal or invent a new one. Just be sure the situation has dramatic potential.

create a believable plot

By now you've selected a situation or invented one of your own. You've decided that it has a conflict with dramatic potential. And you're ready to develop the situation into a scenario, an outline of a plot. Your scenario is your map. It shows you a starting point, a route, and a destination for your play. The starting point is the conflict. The destination, the way you resolve the conflict.

The first step is to think about the conflict. Let's say you've decided to work with one of the situations suggested in the previous lesson. You've decided to build a play on this situation:

> Linda receives a phone call from Paul. He says he loves her, but he can't go through with their marriage, which is scheduled to take place in an hour.

As you think about the situation, ask yourself, What happens next? What will Linda do about the news she has just received?

Before you come up with a final answer to this question, you need to think about how you want to treat the situation. Will your play be serious or comic? Do you want to get into heavy drama? Or would you rather write something amusing? Which treatment you choose might depend on how you feel about the situation. What choices does the character have? What could a young woman do in such a predicament? What is she likely to do? What should she do? While you think through the character's problem, you can put yourself or someone you know in Linda's place.

A dramatist . . . should ask himself three questions:
In this situation, what should I do? What would
other people do? What ought to be done?
—Alexandre Dumas

Your first response might be that Linda would be very upset. So you decide to write a serious play showing her coming away from the phone in tears, perhaps telling her bridesmaid about the terrible thing that happened to her. Then you end the play with the bridesmaid trying to comfort Linda. But would this make a good plot? Is the conflict resolved? Haven't you left the audience hanging, still wondering what Linda will do next? You need to show Linda doing something, making a choice. The conflict should be resolved before the play ends.

All right. Suppose that after trying to comfort Linda, the bridesmaid leaves. Then you show Linda writing a farewell note, reading it aloud (so that your audience will know what she has written), and then packing her suitcase. She has decided to run away and start her life over again somewhere else. Here Linda is clearly deciding to do something. But there is a danger in this kind of plot. The choice Linda makes is a drastic one. The audience may feel that she is overreacting. You need to resolve the conflict in a way that satisfies your audience, a way that fits their sense of how things happen. Especially in a short play, you might not have time to convince the audience that Linda can solve her problem only by running away.

Maybe you want to try a lighter approach. So you continue the scenario like this:

> Just as Linda hangs up the phone, the doorbell rings. It's Bob, an old boyfriend, who has heard that Linda's getting married to Paul and has come to talk her out of it. Bob grabs the grateful Linda in his arms, and they agree to marry immediately, taking advantage of the preparations that have already been made.

But isn't Bob's arrival too convenient? Here you have dodged the conflict rather than resolved it. The audience will feel let down. Why? For one thing, the outcome of a play is more believable if it depends on the decisions and actions of the main character rather than on a chance event, a coincidence. Secondly, a true happy ending for this situation, one that would satisfy the audience, would have to bring Linda and Paul back together.

The next question is, How can you get Linda and Paul back together? What if, just as Linda is about to run away, Paul arrives and announces that he has thought it over and really wants to marry her after all? Will this resolution satisfy the audience? Why not? Why isn't it believable?

When you think about it, having Paul change his mind like this is an even weaker resolution than having the old boyfriend turn up. Linda still hasn't taken any action to resolve her problem. And, what's worse, this scenario shifts the focus of interest away from Linda and her problem to Paul. The audience will begin to wonder why Paul changed his mind. Or they will see Linda's conflict as unreal and artificial. But is there a way you can bring Linda and Paul back together and still focus your plot on what Linda does to solve her problem? Think about it.

Up to now, all the scenarios you've tried out have had Linda assume that her wedding has fallen through. But suppose Linda sees things differently. Suppose she gives more weight to her belief that Paul still loves her than to his statement that he doesn't want to go through with the wedding. Perhaps she realizes that he's just suffering from a temporary lack of nerve. So what she does is to ask Paul for one last favor. Will he go to the church and spare her the embarrassment of being stranded at the altar? She implies that she'll stay home. Paul agrees. But Linda has no intention of staying home. She goes to the church and faces Paul as though nothing were wrong. And they are married.

Here the focus is on what Linda does. The outcome depends on her decisions and actions. You have one conflict and one main character. Linda takes a cool-eyed view of her problem, and the happy ending is thus believable.

But you can't go directly from the beginning of your play to the end, from introducing the conflict to resolving it. Every play—no matter how short it is—has to have a middle as well. Why? What would happen if you simply introduced your conflict and then resolved it? You need the middle to create suspense, to complicate the situation. If the outcome is completely predictable, the audience will get bored. The complication will point to an outcome different from the one you are planning. In a comedy, it will create false fears that point toward an unhappy ending. In a tragedy, the complication will create false hopes that point toward a happy ending.

How can you create a middle for the play about Linda and Paul? How can you complicate the situation by giving the audience false fear? One way is to make use of a character who misunderstands the situation. Assume that when Linda receives the phone call from Paul, her bridesmaid Jill is with her. Then when Linda asks

Paul to go to the church, Jill could misinterpret Linda's plan. She could think that the wedding is off, and Linda could delay telling her the truth. This way the audience won't be sure just what the outcome is to be. At the time the complication is introduced, the false outcome that it points to should seem believable to the audience. But by the end of the play, the real outcome should seem more believable.

PLOTTING THE ACTION

Read over the situation you've chosen and begin writing a scenario for a short play. Your teacher may want you to do this either as a class project or as an individual assignment. Your first problem is to decide who the main character will be, the one who resolves the conflict. Say you've decided to develop this situation into a scenario:

> Dave's father discovers a duplicate key that Dave has had made for the family car.

You might want to focus on what Dave's father does when he finds the key, how he chooses to solve the problem of what to do or say to Dave. In that case Dave's father would be the main character. Or you might prefer to emphasize Dave's conflict when he realizes that his father must have discovered the key or when his father confronts him with the discovery. Then Dave would be the main character.

You might be writing a play about what happens when two characters hold conflicting opinions. For example, suppose you use the situation in which a husband wants his aged mother to live with him, but his wife thinks the mother should live in a home for the elderly. Again you would have to decide which character will have the more important role in the story. Which one will do or say something that will resolve the conflict? It doesn't matter which character you decide to make the main character. The point is that you can have only one main character, not two characters of equal importance.

Once you've decided exactly what the conflict is and which character should resolve it, jot down the various choices the

Scenario

Situation: Linda gets a call from her
    fiance Paul an hour before her
    wedding. He wants to back out.

What {could, should, would} she do?

1. She could cry. What then? Her
bridesmaid could comfort her.

2. She runs away. Wants to get
away from embarrassing scene.

3. Maybe an old boyfriend could
show up — In THE NICK OF TIME.
Convenient. Too convenient.

4. Just as she's packing her suitcase,
Paul arrives. He's changed his mind
again. Why would he do that?

What kind of person is Linda? Hysterical?
calm, level, smart. What would that kind of
person do?

She could ask Paul to go to the church in
her place. Then she would show up
anyway. Paul would be so glad to see her
they'd go ahead and get married.

Middle? The plot thickens! ??

Linda's bridesmaid overhears the phone
conversation and misunderstands.
Linda keeps her in suspense — and the
audience too!

character has. Decide whether you want to write a serious play or a comedy and select an appropriate outcome. Be sure that the outcome is believable—that it is something that is likely to happen and that it depends on what the main character decides to do. Finally, invent a complication for your plot. Make it something that will create suspense by misleading the audience. If you're planning a happy ending, your complication should create false fears. If an unhappy ending, then false hopes. You'll probably find that you have to go through several drafts before you've completed a scenario you're satisfied with.

from scenario to script

You selected a situation with dramatic potential. You focused on a main character, decided whether the play will be serious or light, and determined how the conflict will be resolved. Finally, you wrote a summary of the actions of your play, a scenario. Now, how do you translate this scenario into dialogue and stage directions?

First, you need to visualize where your play will take place. If you were building a play around the situation of Linda and Paul, where would you set the action? Remember, Linda's conflict arises only an hour before her wedding—when Paul phones her. Where would Linda be then? Probably in her room, getting dressed. So you set the scene in Linda's room, an hour or so before her wedding.

Do you need to describe Linda's room now? No. In fact, the scene description is often better left until last. All you need now is to know where the action takes place. After you've written your dialogue, you'll be in a better position to describe the kind of set your play should have.

When the curtain opens on your play, the characters on the stage will be total strangers to your audience. So your first task is to let the audience know who these people are and what their problem is. And the only way you have of doing this is through dialogue, the speech of the characters. You might begin like this, with Linda and her bridesmaid Jill chatting while they get ready for the wedding:

130

JILL: I can hardly believe it, Linda. Paul Bartlett's getting married at last.

LINDA: I can hardly believe it myself, considering how many girls he's walked out on in the past.

JILL: Why did he keep getting involved with girls he really wasn't interested in?

LINDA: He's just too charming for his own good, that's all. Whenever he was introduced to someone, he tried to show a little interest, act like a human being. . . . Well, there was something about the way he did it that used to make every girl who met him think he was madly in love with her.

JILL: But he really wasn't at all?

LINDA: No, so he'd have to try to get out of the situation.

JILL: And now he's actually getting married . . . to you.

LINDA: I guess I should feel pretty lucky.

JILL: Maybe it's just that he realizes you're the one girl for him.

LINDA: Maybe that's it. He's certainly the only man for me.

JILL: Just how did you and Paul get together, Linda?

LINDA: We met last summer. On the beach at Cape Cod.

JILL: That's when you were working at that lab in Woods Hole, wasn't it?

LINDA: Right. Paul was on vacation there. Funny thing, we grew up in the same small town, but we never got to know each other until after we had left.

JILL: And just think. In one hour you'll be Mrs. Paul Bartlett.

(*Sound of telephone ringing.*)

All right, this dialogue gives the audience the background information they need to understand the situation. That's one thing the dialogue at the beginning of your play must accomplish. But dialogue shouldn't sound like explanation. And that's what this dialogue sounds like. It's just a series of remarks, without the give-and-take of natural conversation. These lines could all have been said by one person. There is no interplay of personalities or feelings. It's obvious that Linda and Jill are discussing things they already know just for the benefit of the audience. Linda does all the explaining, while Jill feeds questions to Linda for no reason or just echoes things Linda says.

What should you do to make the dialogue more lifelike? To begin with, you have to see your characters as individuals. You have to make them different from each other in some important way. Why? When you're writing a play, the best way to get something across to the audience is to show it in contrast to something else.

> **Contrast is the dramatist's method.**
> **—Lord Dunsany**

It is important, for example, for the outcome of the play about Linda and Paul that Linda be calm and cool. So why not make the bridesmaid Jill excitable and sentimental? Then you have a contrast. Perhaps Linda is flippant and sarcastic while Jill takes everything too literally. Maybe she and Linda don't get on too well. You can show their personalities clashing on stage.

To show the contrast between your characters, you should write your dialogue from a constantly shifting viewpoint. Get inside each character's head every time she has something to say. Even if it's just yes or no, be sure you know what the character is feeling before you let her say it. Take on her point of view. For example, if Jill is quizzing Linda about her relationship with Paul, ask yourself, Why would she want to know? Maybe she was once interested in Paul. Maybe that interest isn't completely dead. She might even have a few things to tell Linda about Paul.

If you do this, you'll automatically divide the dialogue fairly evenly between the characters. You'll find that they both have interesting things to say. Your dialogue—and your characters, too—will begin to come to life. And the background information will reveal itself naturally.

> **The more that is revealed of situation . . . by the**
> **opening lines of the play, the better. . . . And re-**
> **revealed not by explanation, but by the natural**
> **impulsive speech of the characters telling each**
> **other things they do not know but want to know.**
> **—Rachel Crothers**

Are there any other ways besides contrast to make dialogue more effective? One thing to remember is that the audience gets to hear your dialogue only once. They can't ask the actors to repeat something they didn't understand. So your dialogue has to be clear, clearer than ordinary conversation would be. You have to make sure the important ideas get across.

In the first draft of dialogue between Linda and Jill, too much important information has been crowded into a few lines of dialogue. It's more than the audience could absorb in the short time it would take the actors to speak the lines. The dialogue needs to be longer so that the main ideas can be separated and given emphasis. You do this by extending each idea, taking more time with it.

There are two main ways you can extend an idea through dialogue. One is to lead up to it gradually. For example, you could emphasize the kind of relationship Linda has with Paul by having Jill hesitate to ask questions about it. Have her take time to get to the point. Another way to extend an idea is to linger on it. You can do this by giving examples. For instance, you might have Linda and Jill emphasize Paul's past experiences with women by talking about specific girl friends whom Paul has dropped.

Be sure your characters talk only about things that are important to the play. Don't pad your dialogue with weather talk or jokes. They will stop the flow of the play's action.

> **Each piece of dialogue *must* be "something happening". . . . The "amusing" for its *own* sake should above all be censored. . . . The functional use of dialogue for the plot must be the first thing in the . . . [writer's] mind. Where functional usefulness cannot be established, dialogue must be left out.**
> **—Elizabeth Bowen**

Finally, you can make dialogue more effective if you vary its pace. The first draft of the dialogue between Linda and Jill, for example, moves fairly slowly and monotonously. To make dialogue move more quickly, use shorter speeches, especially questions and answers and interruptions. But don't be afraid to include some longer speeches. You need them to keep the rhythm of your dialogue interesting.

Here's an improved version of the opening dialogue between Linda and Jill. It sounds more lifelike because Linda and Jill have interesting and contrasting personalities. Its main ideas are clearer because they've been spread out and made emphatic. Also, it's well paced. Notice that it includes a few stage directions. These are mostly instructions for the actors—which gesture to make, how to deliver a line, when to leave the stage. Since they are intended for the actors, not the audience, you should separate stage directions from the dialogue by enclosing them in parentheses. But don't try to tell the actors what emotion should accompany every line of dialogue. They will supply their own interpretations of the lines, as you can see from the actor's script on the facing page. Leave something for their imaginations to work on.

> *Scene: Linda's bedroom.*
>
> *As the curtain opens,* Jill *is alone. She's standing in front of a full-length mirror, holding* Linda's *wedding dress in front of her. At the sound of a door closing offstage,* Jill *hastily hangs up the wedding dress.* Linda *comes into the room, carrying the mail—a package and a number of letters and cards.*
>
> JILL: Oh, Linda, it's you. I'm so excited. I've never been a maid of honor before.
>
> LINDA: (*Casually glancing through the letters.*) Then we're even, Jill. I've never been a bride before. (*Continues reading.*)
>
> JILL: Aren't you going to open the package?
>
> LINDA: I don't think so. It's a present from the Meyers. It'll be easier to be polite to them at the reception if I don't know exactly what ugly little knickknack they've chosen.
>
> JILL: You don't seem the least bit excited. Don't you realize what a big occasion this is?
>
> LINDA: In my own way I'm very happy. I just don't think there's any particular reason to get hysterical.
>
> JILL: Just think, you're getting married . . . to Paul Bartlett. . . . Linda?
>
> LINDA: (*Still reading letters.*) Yes?
>
> JILL: There's something I've been wanting to ask you.
>
> LINDA: What is it?
>
> JILL: Well, I'm not quite sure how to ask it.
>
> LINDA: Just blurt it out.
>
> JILL: You're making fun of me.
>
> LINDA: I'm not, really. But if you've got something to ask, ask it.
>
> JILL: I don't want you to think . . .

HALE: (Grasping Abigail.) Abigail, it may be your cousin

is dying. Did you call the Devil last night?

ABIGAIL: I never called him! Tituba, Tituba...

PARRIS: (Blanched.) She called the Devil?

HALE: I should like to speak with Tituba. *stern & abrupt*

PARRIS: Goody Ann, will you bring her up? (Mrs. Putnam

exits.)

HALE: How did she call him?

ABIGAIL: I know not--she spoke Barbados.

HALE: Did you feel any strangeness when she called him?

A sudden cold wind, perhaps? A trembling below the

ground? *frightening her*

ABIGAIL: I didn't see no Devil! (Shaking Betty.) Betty,

wake up. Betty! Betty!

HALE: You cannot evade me, Abigail. Did your cousin

drink any of the brew in that kettle?

ABIGAIL: She never drank it! *X L, around*

HALE: Did you drink it? *bed & sit next to abigail*

ABIGAIL: No, sir!

HALE: Did Tituba ask you to drink it? *start pressing her*

ABIGAIL: She tried, but I refused.

HALE: Why are you concealing? Have you sold yourself

to Lucifer? *harder*

LINDA: Sorry, that's a requirement I can't fulfill.

JILL: Would you be serious for one minute?

LINDA: I'll try.

JILL: You're just like Paul. A person can never hold a real conversation with either of you.

LINDA: Then it's a good thing *I'm* marrying him and not you.

JILL: (*Is shocked, perplexed, then furious.*) I . . . I wouldn't marry Paul Bartlett if he were the last man in the world!

LINDA: That's a pretty heavy protest.

JILL: (*Getting control of herself.*) I don't see how anyone could get Paul to be serious long enough even to consider marriage.

LINDA: So that's what you've been dying to know.

JILL: (*Encouraged.*) How *did* you finally trap him?

LINDA: I didn't *trap* him.

JILL: How can you say that?

LINDA: Because it's true.

JILL: But everyone knows Paul's the cagiest bachelor in town. I don't know how many girls have been after him, and he always slips right out of their grasp. Poor Mary Anne didn't even make it beyond the first date. Paul dropped her because she ate catsup on her steak.

LINDA: Was that the real reason?

JILL: If you think that's a bad reason, you should hear what he told Carol. (*Mimicking.*) "My doctor tells me I'm allergic to the perfume you're wearing."

LINDA: (*Laughing.*) What kind was it?

JILL: *Jungle Gardenia.*

LINDA: Poor Paul. His real problem is that he's just too charming for his own good.

JILL: Charming? I don't call that charming.

LINDA: But he never intended to get involved with those girls. It's just that whenever he got introduced to someone, he tried to show a little interest, ask a few questions, act like a human being. . . . Well, there was something about the way he did that that used to make every girl who met him think he was madly in love with her. But you know what I mean, Jill. . . . Weren't you once interested in Paul?

JILL: (*Obviously lying.*) No, I never thought Paul was the least bit charming.

LINDA: (*Knows she's lying.*) I guess you were more perceptive than the others. Anyway, Paul wasn't really in love with any of them. Each time he had to wiggle out of the situation somehow. This was hard for him because he didn't want to hurt anyone. So he tried to keep it light.

JILL: Maybe you call it light. I call it malicious.

LINDA: Don't say that, Jill. You've got him all wrong. Paul's a very special guy.

JILL: I think he's just plain insensitive.

LINDA: No, if anything, he's too sensitive.

JILL: I can't believe that.

LINDA: Really, he is. But it got him into trouble. So he had to build a shell around himself . . . for protection.

JILL: So how did you break through the shell?

LINDA: I don't really know. Funny thing is that even though Paul and I grew up in the same small town, we never dated, not till last summer at least.

JILL: Last summer? Weren't you on Cape Cod last summer?

LINDA: Right. I had a grant at the oceanographic lab at Woods Hole and—

JILL: Don't tell me you two were brought together by some . . . some fish!

LINDA: It sounds strange, but that's how it happened. Paul was there on vacation. And we just happened to bump into each other on the beach and started talking. He seemed fascinated by what I was doing at the lab and kept asking me all kinds of questions about what fish we were studying and why we were studying them. Honestly, I didn't even realize that Paul was interested in me. I just thought he liked fish. You might say he deceived me.

(*Sound of telephone ringing.*)

In this dialogue between Linda and Jill, the playwright uses the conversation of the two women to prepare the audience for Paul's phone call. But neither Linda nor Jill shows an awareness of the approaching conflict.

In developing your own scenario, you may have to deal with a slightly different situation. Your main character may already be aware of the conflict when the play begins. The problem, however, is the same. You have to explain the conflict to your audience in a way they will accept as being lifelike. To do this, you must see your characters as distinct, usually contrasting, personalities.

SETTING YOUR PLAY IN MOTION

Go back to your scenario. Think where the action will take place. Then begin writing dialogue. See if you can build a contrast between your characters. Show this contrast in the way they discuss their problem. For instance, if you're writing about the situation in which Melva offers Annette answers to the math test, you might show that both Melva and Annette are poor students, but that Annette tries while Melva is lazy. Your dialogue could start out like this:

MELVA: (*Coming into the empty classroom where* Annette *is studying.*) Still hard at work?

ANNETTE: (*Not looking up.*) Go away, Melva.

MELVA: But, Annette. It's nearly five o'clock. They're going to lock you up in the school.

ANNETTE: Good! Maybe then I'll be able to concentrate on this math. I can never get anything done at home.

MELVA: I'm not a bit worried about that test tomorrow. I've got it cinched.

ANNETTE: (*Finally looking up.*) How can you say that? You got 53 on that last test. At least I got a 69. One more point and I would have passed.

MELVA: I'm gonna get a perfect score!

As you continue your play, make your dialogue as lively, clear, and well paced as you can.

onstage or offstage?

Suppose that one of the events in your scenario is a high-speed auto chase. Can you show this happening in your play? Not effectively. It's the kind of action that's physically impossible to put on the stage. It requires far more space than a stage can provide.

There are other actions like this that are just too big for the stage. Battles, for example. To do a realistic battle scene, you need the sweep of a camera over a cast of thousands. It belongs in a movie, not on the stage. So do airplane crashes, sailboat races, football games.

Some events are not impossible to stage. They're just impractical. If most of your play takes place in Karen's living room, you probably would think twice before planning an additional scene showing the junior prom in full swing. Or a scene in a crowded restaurant.

Does this mean that you have to leave these events completely out of your play? No. You may not be able to show them, but you can suggest that they have taken place. Instead of showing a battle scene, you can show soldiers returning from the battle. You can show someone rushing on stage to tell someone else that there's been a plane crash. The morning after the prom, two of your characters can compare notes on who danced with whom.

It's possible to create a lively scene just having characters talk about an event. In fact, showing a character finding out that an event has taken place can sometimes be more striking than showing the event itself.

But this doesn't mean that you should always have your characters talk about events, that you should never show the events themselves. As a rule, put all of the events in your scenario on the stage. By letting the audience see an event happening, you bring it closer to them. You make it vivid. And because the audience can experience it directly, the event will be more believable.

In the play about Linda and Paul, for example, what about the telephone conversation? Does it make any difference whether you show Linda talking on the phone to Paul or have her go offstage to take the call and then report it to Jill?

There is no general rule about telephone calls in plays. It depends on the situation. In this case you want the audience to believe for a while that Linda and Paul's wedding is not going to take place. You've planned in your scenario that Jill will misunderstand the situation so that you can lead the audience astray. Then later Linda will set Jill—and the audience—straight.

So you need to delay Linda's telling Jill her plan to overcome Paul's fears. If Linda takes the phone call offstage and then reports the conversation to Jill, would there be any reason for her not to tell Jill right away what she's planning? No. Of course, you could think up some kind of interruption—the doorbell could ring, the roof could cave in, Jill could faint, Linda could trip on the rug or choke on a peanut. But the audience probably wouldn't buy it. It would seem too contrived. Sending Linda offstage to answer the phone would present another problem. What would you have Jill do while Linda was gone?

If you show the phone conversation taking place, you can solve several problems at once. You can supply your audience with the facts you want them to have, and you can give Jill something to do. And you can use Jill's reaction to the facts to build up tension about the outcome.

Staging the telephone conversation will help make the scene believable. You want to make the audience believe that it's possible to draw two different conclusions from what Linda says to Paul. To do this, you have to let the audience hear the conversation for themselves. Because the outcome of the phone call is to be concealed from the audience, the phone call itself should be out in the open.

True, the audience will hear only what Linda says. But you can create the impression of what Paul is saying. How? First, you have to hear the whole conversation in your imagination, even though you write down only Linda's part in it. If you do this, you can let Linda's responses echo what Paul would be saying. For instance, he might start out by saying, "I want you to know that I really love you." You could get this across by having Linda say, "I'm glad to hear that. I love you too." Be sure to indicate pauses whenever Linda would be listening to Paul. Do this with periods (. . .).

You might even prepare the audience for the telephone conversation by having Jill answer the phone and then tell Linda that Paul sounds strange. During the telephone conversation, have Jill make comments that lead the audience to take on her point of view. The scene might go like this:

> JILL: (*Running to phone before Linda can get to it.*) Hello. . . . Oh, Paul. . . . Just a minute. . . . (*To Linda.*) It's Paul. He sounds kind of strange.
>
> LINDA: Paul? . . . (*Listening, and then warmly, but a little surprised and amused.*) I'm glad to hear that. I love you too.
>
> JILL: So what else is new?
>
> LINDA: (*Even more surprised, but still controlled.*) You don't? . . . Well, I think I know how you feel. Marriage *is* a big step.
>
> JILL: Oh, no. He's backing out again.
>
> LINDA: No, I know it doesn't mean you've stopped loving me. . . . No, Paul, I understand. Really, I *do*. Look, if it makes you feel any better, I've been having some second thoughts myself. So maybe we should just call the whole thing off for the time being.
>
> JILL: No, Linda. Don't let him get away with it.
>
> LINDA: Sure, I have. You don't think you're the only one with doubts, do you? . . . Well, not *too* many. But it takes courage to commit yourself to spend your whole life with another person, no matter how wonderful that person might be.

JILL: Wonderful?

LINDA: Of course, I think you're wonderful. Listen, Paul, I'd like to ask you to do me a favor. Would you go to the church? It would spare me the embarrassment of being stranded at the altar. I hate clichés, and at least no one can say that "Groom stranded at altar" is a cliché! . . . You will? Good. I knew I could count on you. . . . Bye.

By dramatizing the phone call, you have not only made it more believable, you've also made it vivid and memorable. The audience will be able to watch Linda while she is getting the news from Paul and see the difference between her reaction and Jill's. You are giving them a firsthand experience of a crucial moment in the play.

DRAMATIZING ACTIONS

What physical actions does the plot of your play suggest? Show as many of these actions on the stage as you can. They'll make your plot more vivid for the audience and more believable too. But don't show events that are impractical on the stage. Instead, help the audience imagine that they have happened by showing your characters talking about them. Be careful, too, not to have too many changes of scene. The fewer you have, the better.

know when to stop

Suppose you're writing a whodunit. After you've let the audience find out who committed the crime, do you have to show the arrest, then the trial, and finally the sentencing of the criminal? Unless you have a special reason for doing so, the answer is no. All you need to do is show someone calling the police. The audience will assume the rest.

There is a principle involved here, one that applies to all kinds of plays. Once the audience learns what the outcome of the conflict is, the plot is finished. And your play should end as quickly as possible. Especially in a short play, you should not include events that are anticlimactic, that just seem tacked on after the plot is really over.

Where would you end the play about Linda and Paul? Would you end it with the wedding scene? That depends on when the audience learns what the outcome is to be. If you show Linda telling Jill her plan, then you don't need the wedding scene. The audience will take the wedding for granted. And it wouldn't add anything more to the plot. It would be anticlimactic. You would include this scene only if you're planning to have the wedding turn out differently from what Linda expects. Then such a scene would contribute something to the plot.

So, as soon as Linda announces her plan, you must end the play. You can delay her announcement for some time by focusing the audience's attention on what Jill says. You can make Jill upset. Have her try to give Linda advice. Show her complaining about

Paul. Then, when you think your audience will have decided that there is to be no wedding, have Linda tell about her plan. But don't have her announce it all in one speech. That would make the ending of the play too abrupt. You can have her let the information trickle out a little at a time. Why would she do this? Perhaps she enjoys teasing Jill. Then end the play as Linda and Jill leave for the wedding.

JILL: Linda, if you aren't the most cold-blooded person I've ever seen, I don't know who is. First, you weren't even excited about your wedding. And now that it's off, you seem even calmer.

LINDA: Things have a way of working themselves out for the best sometimes.

JILL: How can you say that? Don't you love Paul?

LINDA: Of course I love him.

JILL: Then you should be willing to fight for him.

LINDA: What do you want me to do? Drag him bodily out of his apartment and into the church?

JILL: No, but you could have tried to talk some sense into his head. Argue with him. Beg him to think of you instead of only himself.

LINDA: But then I would be as selfish as you think he is.

JILL: Well, then, you should have started talking about something . . . fish, maybe . . . anything to keep him on the line until you could think of a way to get him to change his mind.

LINDA: Jill, you can't make people do things they're not ready to do.

JILL: Well, what are you going to do? Are you just going to let him get away?

LINDA: Cheer up, Jill. Things aren't as bad as they seem.

JILL: Cheer up! What have I got to cheer up about? Here I am with a new dress—it cost me a hundred dollars—and a new hairdo. And now nobody's even going to see me. And it's all Paul's fault.

LINDA: You'll be seen. Just get that dress on. We've only got twenty minutes!

JILL: Twenty minutes? To what?

LINDA: To get to the church.

JILL: Don't tell me you're actually going to show up at the scene of humiliation.

LINDA: No, I'm going to a scene of triumph.

JILL: Triumph? Whose triumph? Paul's? There should be a headline: "Paul Bartlett Eludes Marriage Once Again!"

LINDA: (*Quietly.*) No, Jill. Love's triumph.

JILL: I don't understand.

LINDA: I want to be there when love triumphs over a very dear man's nervousness.

JILL: But—

LINDA: That's all it is, Jill. Nervousness. Last-minute jitters. It's the formality of the occasion. Paul's more afraid of dropping the wedding ring or stumbling during the ceremony than he is of marriage itself. When he sees that I have come to the church after all, love will give him the courage he needs to get through the day. (*Looks at her watch.*) But if we don't hurry, we won't make it in time.

(*Curtain.*)

There might be other ways to end this play. You could, for instance, add another scene that would show Linda and Jill one year later. But if you did that, you would have to think of a way to keep the audience from learning about the outcome until that scene.

ENDING YOUR PLAY

Think about the outcome of the conflict of the play you are writing. What would be an effective way to let the audience know what the outcome is? You might want to experiment with several different approaches before you decide on one. For practice, perhaps you want to write a different ending for the play about Linda and Paul. You could, for instance, not show Linda telling Jill about her plan before the wedding. Perhaps Linda could just ask Jill to come with her to the church because she wants to prove something to her about Paul. Then you could add a scene between Linda and Jill that would take place one year later. You'd let the audience know what the outcome was at that point.

145

CHOOSING A TITLE

When you've finished writing your play, you need to decide what you're going to call it. What kind of title would be most effective? You want to arouse the audience's interest. And you want to give them some idea of what the play is about. What if you called the play about Linda and Paul *The Reluctant Bridegroom?* There are two things wrong with this title. One is that it gives too much away. Another is that the play is really more about Linda than about Paul. Instead, why not call it *The Phone Call?*

WRITING A SCENE DESCRIPTION

There are several approaches you can take to describing the scene of your play. You might take the practical approach. Think of the simplest possible arrangement of stage set

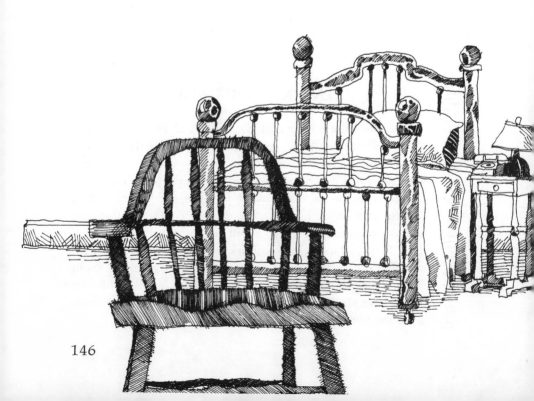

and props that would suggest the place where your play happens. What you write down will be instructions for the set designer. Here's an example of that kind of scene description:

> *The setting is a room in a boarding house, actually the representation of a room—there need be no especial fidelity to reality: a fragment of necessary wall here and there; no doors, only doorways. The bathroom is also visible: a tub, a washbasin, a toilet. A bed is placed with its head against the upper wall; next to it is a small table with a lamp and telephone; there is also a wooden armchair. These are all at stage right. The bathroom is at stage left. The entrance to the room is center, in the upper wall.* —William Hanley

Maybe you would rather write the kind of scene description that's intended for someone who might read your play but who won't see it on the stage. Many playwrights use this approach in the published editions of their plays. You need to describe the scene more fully so the reader can visualize it. And you might want to use scene description to help suggest the emotional atmosphere of the play as well. Here's a scene description that gives the reader a picture of the scene and a feeling for the mood of the play.

> *Place: The Berniers' living room, the entrance porch to the house, and a small city garden off the porch. The house is solid middle-class of another generation. The furniture is heavy and old. Everything inside and outside is neat, but in need of repairs. The porch has two rocking chairs and is crowded with plants. The garden has a table and chairs that have been painted too often and don't stay together very well. It is a house lived in by poor, clean, orderly people who don't like where they live.*
> —Lillian Hellman

Before you decide on a scene description for your own play, try describing Linda's room. Which technique will you use? Do you want to indicate how a very simple setting could suggest Linda's room? Or do you want to describe her room in a way that might reveal her personality? Maybe you want to use one approach for Linda's room and the other for the setting of your own play. It's up to you.

PRESENTING YOUR PLAY

There are many ways you can present your play to an audience. You might want to adapt it for broadcast over a tape recorder. In that case, look through your play to see if you'll need any sound effects to let the audience know what's happening—doors closing, sounds of dishes and silverware during a meal, a telephone ringing. Record these sounds ahead of time so that you're sure you get the effect that you want. Choose some appropriate background music to use during the play or at the beginning and end of the broadcast. Remember, your audience won't be seeing your play. They'll just be hearing it. So check over your scene description. If someone reads it aloud to the audience, will they get a sense of the setting of your play? You might want to make a few changes to make it suitable for broadcast.

You could also create a slide show to visualize the most important moments in your play. Then the actors who read the lines either could be offstage or could sit on one side of the stage.

You might want to try a semistaged production. This can be quite effective. The actors don't need to memorize their lines. And even though they have to hold on to their scripts, they can still go through most of the motions of the play.

Or, if you can persuade the other students in your class to memorize your lines, you can stage your play fully. You might want to serve as director of your own play. Or maybe it would be interesting to see how someone else would translate your script into a production.

Present your play in whatever way appeals to you or seems practical. But, however you present it, make notes on any problems you have with your script during production. Keep track of anything that didn't work on stage. Jot these production notes down in your journal. Then the next time you write a play, you can avoid some of these problems in advance.

6. WRITING A SHORT STORY

a story is a structure

Here's a short story by a high-school student. Read it through to get the sweep of the story. Then be ready to go back over it carefully, so you can see how the writer put it together.

ROLES

Jane was sick and tired of having to defend herself. She wanted to be a pilot; that was that.

As she picked up this month's issue of *Flying* from the library shelf, she could hear Tim chuckling behind her. 5 She looked over at the corner table where he was sitting. He was grinning again. It made her mad. He never came right out and made fun of her. But he got that silly grin on his face every time she mentioned wanting to be a pilot.

She scowled at him and then sat down to read her maga- 10 zine. There was a 747 on the cover. What a beautiful plane. She wondered how it would feel to command a plane of that size. She could just see herself behind the controls. She wouldn't be cold or distant like some pilots of big airplanes on which she'd flown. She'd talk freely on the cabin inter- 15 com, explaining even the little bumps so her passengers would not be afraid.

"Reading about planes again?" Tim was at her side.

"And why not? Since I'm going to be a pilot, I want to know everything I can."

20   "You're sure about that? I mean . . . no doubts?"

"Tim, if you dare laugh at me, I'll never speak to you again. Men! You think a woman couldn't lift one of those giants off the ground. Well, someday soon I'll show you."

"No, it was just that . . . well, I thought you might have
25   some second thoughts by now . . . with graduation coming."

"I do have second thoughts. But they're not about flying. They're about you. Here." She yanked Tim's ring off her finger and banged it on the table.

Tim stared at the ring with its wad of yellow tape. "I
30   don't understand. Are you mad or something?"

But Jane didn't answer. She slapped her magazine back on the rack and rushed out of the library.

When school was over Jane went straight home. She didn't meet Tim at the Snack Shop, as she usually did. She
35   had a math test the next day, and she planned to study all evening. Besides, she never wanted to talk to Tim again—ever. She couldn't stand men who thought they were superior. She'd show him. In fact, she'd even send him a free ticket for her first flight at the controls of a 747.

40   A note was pinned to the bulletin board in her bedroom. It was from her mother, reminding her that she wouldn't be home until nine and that Mrs. Miller expected Jane to baby-sit at six.

How could she have forgotten? And tonight of all
45   nights, when she needed every minute to study for her math test. She had to get a good grade. Pilots had to know their math. Maybe she could get the children bathed and put to bed quickly. If she could get away with it, she might skip their bedtime story.

50   Her mind wandered back to Tim. She remembered the day they met. He seemed like such a sensitive man, not like some guys who didn't care whether a woman had a thought in her head as long as she was cute. They'd met in journalism class and had had a long talk after class

55 about the school paper. She remembered that Tim listened
attentively when she told him she didn't think a school
paper should be a gossip sheet. He agreed and said that he
wanted to write editorials about important issues. His first
published piece had been about the dangers of impurities
60 added to food. Jane had been impressed by his careful
research.

Jane couldn't help looking at her hand. Her finger felt
funny, lighter, with Tim's ring gone. She had grown kind
of used to it. And she had to admit, she had grown kind of
65 used to Tim, too. At times he could really be very thoughtful. She remembered that once he had saved her some
delicious fudge he had helped make for the Track and
Field Club's annual school sale. The fudge was warm and
sweet, and she was so hungry after swim class. Tim could
70 be very considerate that way.

The phone rang, and she guessed it was Tim. She
dreaded having to confront him, even on the phone. She
knew how convincing he could be. She didn't want to be
talked out of her anger. No man was going to make her
75 feel inferior.

"Hello, Jane? Is that you?"

"Yes."

"Would you mind telling me what I did wrong?"

"You've got the nerve to ask that?"

80 "Nerve? Just what did I do anyway?"

"Every time I mention becoming a pilot, you sneer."

"But you don't—"

"I don't have time to argue. Mrs. Miller wants me to
baby-sit."

85 She hung up.

Mrs. Miller had the children dressed and ready for bed.
Thank heavens, Jane thought. *That will save time. If I pop
them in early, I'll have more time to study my math.*

There was a glass of milk and a cookie each for the chil-
90 dren. Jane suddenly realized how hungry she was. No

154

wonder. She hadn't had anything to eat. Well, it was all Tim's fault, really. She was so busy being angry with him she had forgotten to fix herself a quick supper.

95   The children were exhausted. They had spent the afternoon at the circus. They went right to bed and fell asleep almost immediately.

    Jane sat at the dining-room table staring at the cover of her math book. She couldn't concentrate. Math suddenly seemed very dull. And she could hear her stomach growl-
100   ing, low and long. She just couldn't study when she was hungry. But she didn't want to take food from the Millers' refrigerator without permission. Usually Mrs. Miller said, "Help yourself to a snack." But today she had been too rushed even to kiss the children good-bye.

105   The doorbell rang. Jane looked suspiciously out the win- dow. It was Tim.

    "I brought you some hot pizza I just made."

There he was—being thoughtful again, and the smell of the pizza was irresistible.

110 "Eat up. It's my own recipe," he said.

"Your own recipe?" Jane was devouring the pizza.

"Yes. I want to be a cook—a good one. A chef. I thought you'd laugh at me. I guess that's why I kept asking if you were sure about being a pilot. I was trying to . . . well, get
115 confidence from you."

"Tim, I wouldn't laugh at you."

"I'd never laugh at you either."

They both laughed at themselves.

"How about pizza on your first flight? My pizza! And
120 please take this back," Tim said, sliding the ring off his little finger.

There was tomato paste all over the yellow tape. But Jane didn't care. She was too happy.   —Alison Brookston

Suppose someone handed you this story with the incidents all scrambled up—the end at the beginning, the middle at the end, the beginning in the middle. Could you put the story back together again, with everything in the right order? Probably. That's because "Roles" has structure. The incidents are linked together in a definite order. Even the events in the middle of the story have an order.

Where does this structure come from? No one gave the writer of "Roles" a group of prefabricated incidents and said, "Make a story out of these. Use all of them and don't add any others." She had to start from a pretty disorderly collection of events and feelings, some remembered, some imagined, some written down in her journal, and others still chasing one another around inside her head. Until she arranged them into a structure—leaving some out, adding new ones, reshaping others to make them fit—she didn't have a story. Structure is the order that writers give their stories. A story isn't a story until it has structure.

But how can you tell if a story you write has structure? How can you take a disorderly collection of events and feelings and build them into a solid structure?

a story is complete

First of all, to be a solid structure, your story must be complete. That means it has to have all its parts—a beginning, a middle, and an ending.

Your main goal in the beginning section is to alert your readers to the problem your story deals with. Because you're writing a short story instead of a novel, you have to do this immediately. You have to plunge right into the first incident of the story. Novelists can wade slowly into their stories if they want to. They have the time. But short-story writers have to dive in. So don't worry about introductions or explanations. While you're narrating the opening incident, you can also show what your characters are like and how they relate to one another. This is better than explanation. Keep in mind, too, that you don't need an elaborate description of setting. Just be sure that you locate your characters in a specific place. Let your readers see your story as if it were happening in front of their eyes.

Notice how quickly the writer of "Roles" takes you into that story. In the first two sentences, you learn that someone named Jane is tired of having to defend her ambition to become a pilot. Then you find out where she is, what she's doing, and that her boyfriend Tim is causing a problem by seeming to laugh at her ambition. By line 32, Jane has given Tim's ring back to him and rushed out of the library. The opening incident is over, and the story has been launched. The problem posed is this: Is Jane's relationship with Tim in conflict with her plan to become a pilot?

If your goal in the beginning of your story is to present a problem, then your goal in the middle is to create suspense about how that problem is going to be solved. You want to build tension by keeping your readers in doubt. You do this by putting together a string of incidents. Each incident points to either a favorable or an unfavorable solution.

How does this work? In "Roles" the incidents that point—either directly or indirectly—toward Jane and Tim's making up are favorable. Those that point toward their continuing separation are unfavorable. Because the story ends favorably, the unfavorable incidents act as obstacles. They tend to delay the ending of the story. They do this by complicating the situation. On the other hand, the favorable incidents tend to bring the conclusion closer. They simplify.

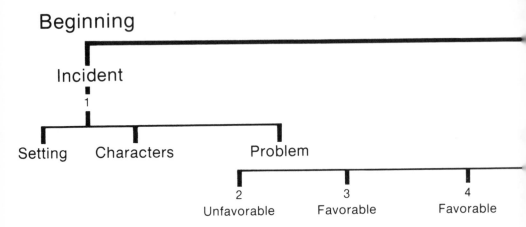

Beginning

Incident

1

Setting   Characters   Problem

2   3   4
Unfavorable Favorable   Favorable

The order of incidents is very important. To create suspense, you have to alternate them. That doesn't mean you can't have two favorable incidents in a row. But the middle of your story should swing back and forth between both kinds of incidents at least twice. Notice how favorable and unfavorable incidents are alternated to build suspense in "Roles." Here's a list of them:

Incident 2 (lines 33–39): Jane's decision not to meet Tim at the Snack Shop continues their separation and is unfavorable.

Incident 3 (lines 41–49): Jane's discovery that she has to baby-sit momentarily frustrates her plan to study math. This discovery works against the goal (becoming a pilot) for which she has broken with Tim. It is therefore indirectly favorable to her relationship with Tim.

Incident 4 (lines 50–70): Jane daydreams about Tim. She remembers that he impressed her when they first met in journalism class. She notices that her hand feels lighter without his ring. And she recalls the time he was thoughtful enough to bring her fudge after her swimming class. These memories and sensations function as a strongly favorable incident. They are so favorable that when the phone rings (line 71) and Jane guesses that it's Tim, we almost expect them to make up right then.

Incident 5 (lines 71–85): The phone call turns out to be unfavorable partly because Jane is in a hurry. In fact, the phone call gives the story a strong push in the direction of continued separation for Jane and Tim.

Incident 6 (lines 86–96): When Jane arrives at the Millers, she dis-

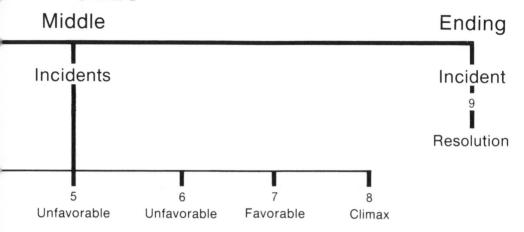

Middle	Ending

Incidents   Incident

9

Resolution

5	6	7	8
Unfavorable	Unfavorable	Favorable	Climax

covers that she'll be able to study her math after all because the children she's taking care of are tired and go right to bed. This is another indirectly unfavorable incident. Separation and independence seem to be winning out.

Incident 7 (lines 97–104): When Jane begins to study, she finds that she is so hungry she can't concentrate. Here Jane, the pilot–math student, doesn't seem to be faring very well. With this incident, the story again leans toward a favorable solution, but only in an indirect way.

Incident 8 (lines 105–109): The final incident in the middle of a story is the climax. Usually this is the most intense of all the incidents. After the climax the solution to the story must follow. Otherwise, it's not the climax. In "Roles" the climax occurs in lines 105–109. Tim arrives, thoughtfully bringing pizza, just when Jane is very hungry. This puts Jane on the spot. What kind of solution will follow? Will Jane and Tim make up? Or will Tim's arrival make Jane even angrier? The events in a climax hang in the balance until they are resolved by the story's ending.

The ending of your story has to solve the problem you raised in the beginning, either favorably or unfavorably. The solution often involves a surprise of some kind, as in the ending of "Roles." But it's not enough just to surprise the reader. The solution must be a logical development of the story. The final incident of "Roles" (*Incident 9*, lines 110–123) makes it clear that Jane can enjoy both her ambition to be a pilot and her relationship with Tim. The conflict that she felt between these two desires was based on a misunderstanding. Tim was never laughing at her. He was just unsure about his own ambition to be a chef.

a story is well proportioned

A story has to be complete. What else? It must have proportion. First, the three parts of a story—beginning, middle, and ending—must be in proportion to one another. "Roles" has excellent proportions. The beginning section is at least twice as long as the ending. And the middle is roughly twice as long as the beginning and the ending combined. At this point, you may be wondering if it's really necessary to measure the parts of your story. No, not if you have an instinct for story proportions. And many writers do. But if you don't think consciously about the proportions of your story, there's a danger that you'll make the beginning too long and then skimp on the middle section. Even the great short-story writer Chekhov felt he had to guard against this tendency. He once wrote to a friend:

> I let myself go at the beginning and write with an easy mind, but by the time I get to the middle I begin to grow timid and to fear my story will be too long. . . . That is why the beginning of my stories is always very promising and looks as though I were starting on a novel, and the middle is huddled and timid, and the end is . . . like fireworks.
> —Anton Chekhov

The time to worry about whether or not your story is getting too long is when you're writing the beginning—or revising the first draft of it. Be selective. Don't include any more detail than you absolutely need to get the story going. When you get to the middle, however, you can be generous with incidents, as was the writer of "Roles." Seven of the nine incidents in "Roles" are found in the middle section. The beginning and the ending have only one incident apiece.

The incidents that make up the middle of your story also have to have proportion. Of the seven incidents in the middle of "Roles," four are favorable and three unfavorable. Since the story ends with Jane and Tim getting together again, it's not surprising that the favorable incidents outnumber the unfavorable. It's clear that if the writer had put in too many unfavorable incidents, she wouldn't have been able to bring the story to a favorable conclusion.

160

What would have happened if the writer had put in nearly all favorable incidents? If she had done that, there would have been no obstacles in the story's path, no resistance to Jane and Tim's coming back together again. When a story moves too easily toward its conclusion—whether favorable or unfavorable—it's really no story at all. It's about as interesting as a barrel rolling straight downhill. For that reason, you need to keep the favorable and unfavorable incidents in the middle of your story almost equal. You should tip the scale only slightly in the direction your story will finally take.

a story is compact

Finally, to be a solid structure, a story must be compact. That means that *every* incident in the story must point to either a favorable or an unfavorable solution to the problem presented by the beginning of the story.

There's no room in a short story for incidents that merely tell something else a character did that day. For example, the writer of "Roles" doesn't show Jane going to class after she leaves the library, even though that would probably be the next thing Jane would do. Instead, the writer skips to an incident that relates to the story's problem. She skips to Jane's decision not to meet Tim at the Snack Shop.

Nor is there room for incidents that only add details of characterization, even interesting details. For example, there wouldn't be room in "Roles" for an incident that shows that Jane is also interested in music.

So make your story complete, well proportioned, and compact. Then it will be a solid structure. And it can have the effect you want it to have.

> The effect produced by a short story depends almost entirely on its form.
>
> —Edith Wharton

COMPARING STORY OPENINGS

Here are ten story openings. Some are taken from short stories, some from novels. Which ones do you think were written by short-story writers trying to make immediate contact with their stories? Which show the more leisurely approach available to a novelist? Why do you think so? Be ready to discuss your reasons in class.

"What will we do now?" said the adjutant, troubled and excited.

"Bury him," said Timothy Lean.

The two officers looked down close to their toes where lay the body of their comrade. The face was chalk-blue; gleaming eyes stared at the sky.   *—Stephen Crane*

When I take a long look at my life, as though from outside, it does not appear particularly happy. Yet I am even less justified in calling it unhappy.   *—Herman Hesse*

A rather small young man sat by the window of a pretty seaside cottage trying to persuade himself that he was reading the newspaper.   *—D. H. Lawrence*

María Concepción walked carefully, keeping to the middle of the white dusty road, where the maguey thorns and the treacherous curved spines of organ cactus had not gathered so profusely. She would have enjoyed resting for a moment in the dark shade by the roadside, but she had no time to waste drawing cactus needles from her feet. Juan and his chief would be waiting for their food in the damp trenches of the buried city.

  —Katherine Anne Porter

My father's family name being Pirrip, and my Christian name Philip, my infant tongue could make of both names nothing longer or more explicit than Pip. So, I called myself Pip, and came to be called Pip.   *—Charles Dickens*

When he was nearly thirteen, my brother Jem got his arm badly broken at the elbow. When it healed, and Jem's fears of never being able to play football were assuaged, he was seldom self-conscious about his injury. His left arm was somewhat shorter than his right; when he stood or walked, the back of his hand was at right angles to his body, his thumb parallel to his thigh. He couldn't have cared less, so long as he could pass and punt.

When enough years had gone by to enable us to look back on them, we sometimes discussed the events leading to his accident. I maintain that the Ewells started it all, but Jem, who was four years my senior, said it started long before that. He said it began the summer Dill came to us, when Dill first gave us the idea of making Boo Radley come out.

—*Harper Lee*

I knew it. I knew if I came to this dinner, I'd draw something like this baby on my left. They've been saving him up for me for weeks. Now, we've simply got to have him— his sister was so sweet to us in London; we can stick him next to Mrs. Parker—she talks enough for two.

—*Dorothy Parker*

After the hurried good-bys the door had closed and they sat at the table with the tragic wreck of the Thanksgiving turkey before them, their heads turned regretfully toward the young folks' laughter in the hall.

—*Ralph Ellison*

I wasn't born yet so it was Cousin Gowan who was there and big enough to see and remember and tell me afterward when I was big enough for it to make sense. That is, it was Cousin Gowan plus Uncle Gavin or maybe Uncle Gavin rather plus Cousin Gowan.　　　—*William Faulkner*

"Present it in a pitiful light," Olson was saying, as they picked their way through the mud toward the orderly room tent.　　　—*Irwin Shaw*

VARYING THE BEGINNING

Try writing a different opening for "Roles." Instead of beginning with Jane's thoughts, you might start out by setting the scene and describing the characters' actions. Or you could get the story started with a terse exchange of dialogue between Jane and Tim. And then you could bring in the other elements, telling what Jane is thinking, where Jane and Tim are, and what they're doing. Maybe you want to use one of the short-story openings in the previous activity as a model. Keep in mind that even though you're trying a different approach, your goal is still the same. You want to plunge the readers into the story. And you need to give them enough information so that they can understand the story as they go along. Compare your opening for "Roles" with the original. Is the effect the same? Different? How? Which opening do you think is better, yours or the original? Why?

SUMMARIZING YOUR STORY IDEA

Now's the time to begin writing your short story. More than likely, you'll need at least two drafts to bring it to a final, polished state. But even before you get going on the rough draft, try writing a fairly detailed summary of your story idea, like that on the opposite page.

As you go through the process of writing a short story, you'll build on this summary. You may convert a sentence from the summary to several lines of dialogue in the rough draft. An adjective may be expanded to a scene description. You might

Story Summary

Jane wants a career—something untraditional for women. She wants to be an airline pilot. Her boyfriend Tim also wants an unusual career. He wants to be a chef. Jane is the direct type and tells Tim about her plan. Tim is uncertain. He doesn't talk to Jane about becoming a chef. When Tim asks her questions about being a pilot, Jane thinks he's laughing at her and she gets mad. He's really just nervous. He looks up to her and is trying to get confidence from her. Jane breaks off their relationship. Tim doesn't understand why. They don't get back together until Tim realizes why Jane is angry and tells her about his career plans.

even go back to Chapter 4 and read through it quickly. This will help to refresh your memory of the steps involved in developing a narrative.

STRUCTURING YOUR STORY

Write a rough draft of your story. Make it a complete structure —with a beginning, a middle, and an ending. Be sure that your beginning poses a problem. If you find that the beginning is getting too long, it may be that you have too much story, perhaps too many characters. Keep it simple. Or maybe you're just taking too long to get into the story. Are you including any background details that the reader doesn't really need to know?

Keep in mind that the middle should be the longest section, at least twice as long as the beginning and the ending put together. That means you'll need to spend most of your time on this section. As you develop incidents for the middle, arrange them to build tension. Alternate incidents that point to a favorable solution to the story's problem with those that point to an unfavorable solution. Include only incidents that relate to this problem. Be sure that your ending provides a satisfying solution to the problem raised by the beginning of the story.

prepare for the ending

An effective surprise ending will at first seem surprising. Then, on second thought, it won't be surprising at all. On second thought it will turn out to be a development that fits naturally into the story.

Good surprise endings don't happen by chance. They take careful preparation on the part of the writer.

First, you have to know just what it is that you're preparing. For that reason, many writers like to write the endings of their stories first.

> **If I didn't know the ending of a story, I wouldn't begin. I always write my last lines, my last paragraph, my last page first, and then I go back and work towards it. I know where I'm going. I know what my goal is.**
>
> **—Katherine Anne Porter**

The surprise ending in "Roles" is based on the sudden revelation of two facts about Tim. First, Jane and the reader find out that Tim is planning to be a chef. Then, they learn that he has not been making fun of Jane after all. He has only been trying to gain enough confidence from her example to admit that he wants to be a chef.

Once you know what your surprise ending will be, then you can plant clues along the way in your story to prepare your readers. But the clues shouldn't be too obvious. After all, you don't want to give away your ending. You need the kind of clue that can be understood in two ways. What kind of clue is that?

Take another look at "Roles." For clues, notice that the writer has planted two incidents in the story that show Tim's interest in food and cooking ahead of time. But she made them both show something else about Tim. The article Tim wrote about impurities in food illustrated his serious attitude toward journalism. And when Tim brought Jane fudge he had made for the Track and Field Club sale, it showed how considerate he was. Only at the end of the story do you discover that these details are, in fact, clues. Only on second thought do you realize that these details are also intended to suggest that Tim wants to be a chef.

Notice, too, that the writer varied the incidents. Only one indicates that Tim has been cooking. The other has him writing an article. If there had been two cooking incidents, the surprise would probably have been given away ahead of time.

Are these the only clues the writer uses to prepare her readers for the surprise ending? What about Tim's chuckling and grinning every time Jane mentions that she wants to be a pilot? And the questions Tim asks her? Aren't these also clues? Can't they be understood in two ways? Jane interprets them one way—that Tim is making fun of her. And you accept Jane's interpretation. But at the end of the story, Jane and you find that Jane's interpretation was based on a misunderstanding.

Tim's chuckling and grinning were just signs of his rather nervous admiration of Jane. But to Jane it seemed that he was making fun of her. When Tim kept asking Jane if she had doubts or second thoughts, he was really trying to find out if she felt any of the insecurity that he felt. But Jane interpreted these questions as criticisms. And when Tim insisted—first in the library and then later on the phone—that he didn't understand why Jane was angry, he didn't realize she thought he was laughing at her. But to Jane it seemed that Tim couldn't understand why it was wrong to laugh at her ambition to be a pilot. Finally, when Tim said, "But you don't—" on the phone, it meant that he suddenly understood the whole situation and was about to explain. But Jane didn't realize this and cut him off impatiently.

Notice how careful the writer was to make Tim's behavior fit Jane's interpretation during the story and Tim's own explanation of it at the end. It works both ways. The readers are misled so they can be surprised. Yet the clues are there to make the surprise seem a natural development of the story.

CREATING INCIDENTS

For practice in creating incidents, experiment with the story "Roles."

Write a short incident that might go somewhere in the middle of "Roles." It could be something that involves Jane in another encounter with Tim. Perhaps she could run into him after school by accident. Or maybe you could have Jane walk home with someone else who talks about Tim. Or you might think of another incident that Jane remembers when she's daydreaming about Tim. Or a completely different incident.

Just be sure that it fits into the structure of the story as either a favorable or an unfavorable incident. It should point either toward Jane and Tim's getting back together or toward their continuing separation.

If you can, try to plant a clue in your incident. It could be something that relates to Tim's interest in food and cooking but also shows another aspect of Tim. Or it could be something Tim says or does that shows he's insecure about becoming a chef but that Jane thinks means he's laughing at her.

Try to find a way to work your incident into the existing story. After you've written your addition, read it carefully in the context of the story. Does it fit? Does it make the story better? Worse? Instead of adding it to the story, try using it to replace one of the incidents already in the story. Which incident makes a better contribution to the structure of the story, yours or the original?

PLANNING THE SURPRISE ENDING

Go back to the story you're writing. Read it straight through. Don't stop to make any corrections. (Be sure you've let at least a day go by since you wrote the first draft. Otherwise, you'll still be too close to your story to experience its effect.) After you've finished reading, think about the way your story ends. Is the ending something startling that just seems tacked on like an afterthought? Or is it already very obvious early in your story what the ending will be?

If you've answered yes to the first question, then you need to prepare your ending better. First of all, make sure that your ending really answers the question raised by the beginning of the story—either favorably or unfavorably. Then write down exactly what the surprise is in your ending. Is it a fact that comes out only at the end? Does a misunderstanding suddenly get cleared up? Now go through your story to see if you have given your readers any clues to this surprise. If not, plant some in the story. Make them fit naturally so they don't stand out like neon signs. Vary them so they won't give the ending away.

If you've answered yes to the second question, then your story probably has clues, but they may be too obvious. Or maybe you have too many clues. Or you may not have enough incidents in the middle of your story that serve as obstacles or complications. Your story may be rolling too smoothly to its conclusion. Revise your story so that the ending really does come as a surprise at first. Then, on second thought, it can seem like a logical development of the story.

choose a point of view

Who is the narrator of "Roles"? Who is telling the story? Is it one of the characters, Jane or Tim? An easy way to find the answer is to look at the pronouns. If a story is told by someone who keeps saying "I," then the narrator is a character in the story. But the narrator of "Roles" never says "I." The narrator of "Roles" is someone who stands outside the story, invisible to the readers, reporting that "she" did this and "he" did that.

But is the narrator of "Roles" only an observer, only someone who watches what happens and listens to what is said? Look again. Right at the beginning of the story, the narrator makes you aware of what's going on inside Jane's head, shows you her thoughts and her feelings. What about Tim? The narrator doesn't show you what Tim is thinking and feeling. Jane is the only character whose thoughts and feelings are revealed. In fact, the narrator tells the story as it is experienced by Jane. Tim is revealed only by what he says and does and by Jane's interpretation of his behavior.

169

This is how most short stories are told. They're written from the third-person point of view with the narrator showing you what's going on inside the mind of one of the characters, usually the main character. It's probably the easiest way to tell a story, and maybe the best. Why?

Flexibility is one reason that so many short stories are told in this way. You'll find that it's easy to move out of the mind of the main character when you need to describe an action or what another character says. Then you can move right back into the character's mind without spoiling the illusion of reality.

What's more, by showing what only one character thinks and feels, you can help to keep your story in sharp focus. You give it a unified effect. If you were to use a narrator who is omniscient, one who enters the mind of each character, you would probably end up with too much detail. The focus of your story would be fuzzy and scattered. Remember, the short story is a brief, compact form. You're much better off to let one character's thoughts and feelings lead the readers through your story.

> **Any rapidly enacted episode . . . should be seen through only one pair of eyes.**
> **—Edith Wharton**

What if you're writing a story that doesn't require that you deal with the inner life of any of your characters? In that case, you can still use third person. But you should be careful to restrict your narrator to the outside of your characters. Here is part of a short story that uses this method:

> Outside the arc light shone through the bare branches of a tree. Nick walked up the street beside the car tracks and turned at the next arc light down a side street. Three houses up the street was Hirsch's rooming house. Nick walked up the two steps and pushed the bell. A woman came to the door.
>
> "Is Ole Andreson here?"
>
> "Do you want to see him?"
>
> "Yes, if he's in."
>
> Nick followed the woman up a flight of stairs and back to the end of a corridor. She knocked on the door.

"Who is it?"

"It's somebody to see you, Mr. Andreson," the woman said.

"It's Nick Adams."

"Come in."

Nick opened the door and went into the room. Ole Andreson was lying on the bed with all his clothes on. He had been a heavyweight prizefighter and he was too long for the bed. He lay with his head on two pillows. He did not look at Nick.

"What is it?" he asked.

"I was up at Henry's," Nick said, "and two fellows came in and tied up me and the cook, and they said they were going to kill you."
—*Ernest Hemingway*

This story, "The Killers," is told from the third-person point of view. But the narrator does not reveal the feelings and thoughts of any of the characters. Basically, what you have is scene description, physical movement, and dialogue. The story approaches drama, the most objective of all forms of fiction.

What if you want your story to sound like someone's personal experience? Then you should tell it in first person. This doesn't mean that you're going to write about yourself. It simply means that you're going to use one of your characters to tell the story. Here's part of a story told from the first-person point of view:

> I can't help it, I'm crazy about thoroughbred horses. I've always been that way. When I was ten years old and saw I was growing to be big and couldn't be a rider I was so sorry I nearly died. Harry Hellinfinger in Beckersville, whose father is Postmaster, is grown up and too lazy to work, but likes to stand around in the street and get up jokes on boys like sending them to a hardware store for a gimlet to bore square holes and other jokes like that. He played one on me. He told me that if I would eat a half a cigar I would be stunted and not grow any more and maybe could be a rider. I did it. When Father wasn't looking I took a cigar out of his pocket and gagged it down some way. It made me awful sick and the doctor had to be sent for, and then it did no good. I kept right on growing. It was a joke. When I told what I had done and why most fathers would have whipped me but mine didn't.
>
> —*Sherwood Anderson*

How can you judge whether a story is better told in third person or in first person? Experiment. Try writing your story from different points of view. For practice, you might even rewrite a professional's story from a different point of view. Then compare the two versions. Which one do you like better? Try to figure out why.

Suppose, for example, that you rewrote the excerpt from Sherwood Anderson's story in third person. It might read like this:

> He couldn't help it, he was crazy about thoroughbred horses. He had always been that way. When he was ten years old and saw he was growing to be big and couldn't be a rider he was so sorry he nearly died. Harry Hellinfinger in Beckersville, whose father was Postmaster, was grown up and too lazy to work, but liked to stand around in the street and get up jokes on boys like sending them to a hardware store for a gimlet to bore square holes and other jokes like that. He played one on the boy. He told him that if he would eat a half a cigar he would be stunted and not grow any more and maybe could be a rider. The boy did it. When his father wasn't looking he took a cigar out of his

pocket and gagged it down some way. It made him awful sick and the doctor had to be sent for, and then it did no good. He kept right on growing. It was a joke. When he told what he had done and why most fathers would have whipped him but his didn't.

In comparing the two versions, what's your strongest impression? It's probably that the original, the one told in first person, is more immediate, more direct. The writer was even able to use the present tense. The second version, on the other hand, probably seems somewhat remote, less lively. Here the third-person point of view puts the reader a step from the action. The character is no longer telling his own story.

The first-person point of view does have the advantage of immediacy. It involves the reader more directly. But it also has an offsetting limitation. If you use it, you are restricted to the thoughts and feelings and observations of the "I" who is telling the story. You can't put anything into the story that the "I" wouldn't notice or experience or, in some way, be able to tell about. This makes it harder to describe external details.

Because of this limitation, you should use the first-person point of view only when you have a special reason for it. One reason might be that you've imagined the "I" of your story as a character who has an interesting, colorful personality. Your plan is that the way "I" tells the story will be as interesting as the story itself. Your "I" might be someone who can talk entertainingly about himself—the way the "I" of the Sherwood Anderson story does. In that case, "I" would be the main character in your story. Or you could use a minor character "I." This would be a character who has a special reason for telling a story about someone else.

Since the third-person and the first-person points of view both have advantages and limitations, why not use both in a short story? Why not switch from one to the other whenever you feel like it? If you were writing a novel, you could probably do this. You can write one chapter in first person and another in third. But in a short story, even a long short story, switching back and forth this way would be very distracting. Your reader would become more aware of the different narrators, the persons telling the story, than of the story itself. The rule to follow is to adopt a point of view at the beginning of a story and stick to it throughout.

GIVING "ROLES" A NEW POINT OF VIEW

Try rewriting "Roles" from one of the following points of view:

1. Let Jane tell the story directly in first person.
2. Have a minor character, someone who knows Jane or Tim or both of them, tell the story in first person.
3. Use a third-person narrator who tells what Tim is thinking but not what Jane is thinking.
4. Have Tim tell the story in first person.
5. Use a third-person narrator who does not reveal the thoughts and feelings of either Jane or Tim.

Your teacher may wish to assign each viewpoint to several students. That way you can compare results.

Keep in mind that the new point of view offers you new possibilities in writing the story. Try to take advantage of them.

You may have to change the story somewhat in order to adjust to the point of view. For example, if you have Jane tell the story in first person, it might be easier to have her tell it as something she remembers. To have her tell it while it is happening would be awkward—though not impossible. If you show what Tim is thinking during the story, you'll still have to find a way to keep the reader from catching on to the surprise ending. Maybe you could have Tim be so upset by Jane's actions that he spends all his time trying to figure her out. If you have a minor

POINT OF VIEW

Third-Person Narrator
(not a character in story)

Omniscient   Dramatic

character tell the story, you'll need to think of a reason why that character would want to tell the story, and you'll need to decide how that character gets the information needed to tell it. Remember, a minor-character narrator won't be able to read Jane's or Tim's mind.

SELECTING ONE POINT OF VIEW

Read the beginning of the story you've been working on. What kind of narrator are you using? Third person? First person?

If your story is written in third person, does the narrator enter the mind of one character? More than one character? Or is the narrator an observer who doesn't read any of the characters' minds?

If your story is written in first person, is the main character doing the telling or a minor character?

Once you've decided which kind of narrator you've used, read through the rest of your story. Think about how the story is being told. Do you think you've made a good choice? Or do you think your story might be better if you rewrite it from a different point of view? Think about the advantages and limitations of each point of view. Sometimes, the only way you can find out which point of view works best for your story is to try out several. Other times, you might realize right away

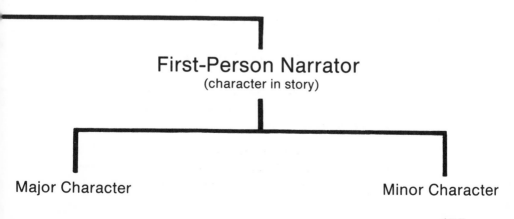

First-Person Narrator
(character in story)

Major Character   Minor Character

that a certain point of view won't work. If, for example, your main character is to die at the end of the story, it would not be a good idea for that character to tell the story in first person as a remembered experience.

Once you have chosen your point of view, make sure you stick to it. Don't switch around. Don't show what a character is thinking if the narrator isn't supposed to be able to read the character's mind. Keep asking yourself, "What kind of narrator is telling this story?" That way, you'll keep your point of view consistent.

what about science fiction?

Suppose you don't want to write a short story about the ordinary world. You'd like to try something a little far-out. Maybe science fiction.

How is a science-fiction story different from a conventional story? It's not all that different. Even a far-out story has to have structure. It has to have the same parts in the same order—a beginning, a middle, and an ending. It should be well proportioned and compact. You still need to plant clues to prepare your readers for the ending. And you need to choose a point of view from which to tell the story.

What's different is the setting. Many, if not most, science-fiction stories take place in the future. The writer imagines a future that is different from the present in some significant way. The events of the story have to be ones that can take place in that futuristic setting.

Here's a story by Isaac Asimov set in the year 2155. What's different about 2155? For one thing, teachers have been replaced by machines.

THE FUN THEY HAD

Margie even wrote about it that night in her diary. On the page headed 17 May, 2155, she wrote, "Today Tommy found a real book!"

It was a very old book. Margie's grandfather once said that when he was a little boy *his* grandfather told him that there was a time when all stories were printed on paper.

They turned the pages, which were yellow and crinkly, and it was awfully funny to read words that stood still instead of moving the way they were supposed to—on a screen, you know. And then, when they turned back to the page before, it had the same words on it that it had had when they read it the first time.

"Gee," said Tommy, "what a waste. When you're through with the book, you just throw it away, I guess. Our television screen must have had a million books on it and it's good for plenty more. I wouldn't throw *it* away."

"Same with mine," said Margie. She was eleven and hadn't seen as many telebooks as Tommy had. He was thirteen.

She said, "Where did you find it?"

"In my house." He pointed without looking, because he was busy reading. "In the attic."

"What's it about?"

"School."

Margie was scornful. "School? What's there to write about school? I hate school." Margie always hated school, but now she hated it more than ever. The mechanical teacher had been giving her test after test in geography and she had been doing worse and worse until her mother had shaken her head sorrowfully and sent for the County Inspector.

He was a round little man with a red face and a whole box of tools with dials and wires. He smiled at her and gave her an apple, then took the teacher apart. Margie had hoped he wouldn't know how to put it together again, but he knew how all right and after an hour or so, there it was again, large and black and ugly with a big screen on which all the lessons were shown and the questions were asked. That wasn't so bad. The part she hated most was the slot where she had to put homework and test papers. She always had to write them out in a punch code they made her learn when she was six years old, and the mechanical teacher calculated the mark in no time.

The Inspector had smiled after he was finished and patted her head. He said to her mother, "It's not the little girl's fault, Mrs. Jones. I think the geography sector was geared a little too quick. Those things happen sometimes. I've slowed it up to an average ten-year level. Actually, the overall pattern of her progress is quite satisfactory." And he patted Margie's head again.

Margie was disappointed. She had been hoping they would take the teacher away altogether. They had once taken Tommy's teacher away for nearly a month because the history sector had blanked out completely.

So she said to Tommy, "Why would anyone write about school?"

Tommy looked at her with very superior eyes. "Because it's not our kind of school, stupid. This is the old kind of school that they had hundreds and hundreds of years ago." He added loftily, pronouncing the word carefully, "Centuries ago."

Margie was hurt. "Well, I don't know what kind of school they had all that time ago." She read the book over his shoulder for a while, then said, "Anyway, they had a teacher."

"Sure they had a teacher, but it wasn't a *regular* teacher. It was a man."

"A man? How could a man be a teacher?"

"Well, he just told the boys and girls things and gave them homework and asked them questions."

"A man isn't smart enough."

"Sure he is. My father knows as much as my teacher."

"He can't. A man can't know as much as a teacher."

"He knows almost as much I betcha."

Margie wasn't prepared to dispute that. She said, "I wouldn't want a strange man in my house to teach me."

Tommy screamed with laughter, "You don't know much, Margie. The teachers didn't live in the house. They had a special building and all the kids went there."

"And all the kids learned the same thing?"

"Sure, if they were the same age."

"But my mother says a teacher has to be adjusted to fit the mind of each boy and girl it teaches and that each kid has to be taught differently."

"Just the same they didn't do it that way then. If you don't like it, you don't have to read the book."

"I didn't say I didn't like it," Margie said quickly. She wanted to read about those funny schools.

They weren't even half finished when Margie's mother called, "Margie! School!"

Margie looked up. "Not yet, Mama."

"Now," said Mrs. Jones. "And it's probably time for Tommy, too."

Margie said to Tommy, "Can I read the book some more with you after school?"

"Maybe," he said, nonchalantly. He walked away whistling, the dusty old book tucked beneath his arm.

Margie went into the schoolroom. It was right next to

her bedroom, and the mechanical teacher was on and waiting for her. It was always on at the same time every day except Saturday and Sunday, because her mother said little girls learned better if they learned at regular hours.

The screen was lit up, and it said: "Today's arithmetic lesson is on the addition of proper fractions. Please insert yesterday's homework in the proper slot."

Margie did so with a sigh. She was thinking about the old schools they had when her grandfather's grandfather was a little boy. All the kids from the whole neighborhood came, laughing and shouting in the schoolyard, sitting together in the schoolroom, going home together at the end of the day. They learned the same things so they could help one another on the homework and talk about it.

And the teachers were people . . .

The mechanical teacher was flashing on the screen: "When we add the fractions ½ and ¼—"

Margie was thinking about how the kids must have loved it in the old days. She was thinking about the fun they had.

—*Isaac Asimov*

In 2155, a teacher is a machine rather than a person. What else is different? Each pupil has a teacher in a schoolroom at home. The pupil writes assignments and tests in a punch code and puts them in a slot in the teacher. The teacher can be speeded up or slowed down to keep pace with the pupil. People read telebooks. Books as we know them are curiosities from the past that someone might happen to find in an attic.

That's really all that's different. If other things are different, too, Asimov doesn't bring them up. He limits himself to details that relate directly to the story he wants to tell.

When you're planning your science-fiction story, you don't need to imagine everything that might possibly be different at some point in the future. Stick to one main difference, as Asimov did. That will make it easier to focus your story.

One way to begin your story is to think of a particular problem that needs solving. Asimov may have been thinking of the need for individual teaching. After that, imagine a solution to your problem.

You might imagine a solution to a medical problem, for example. Suppose people of the future could provide themselves with body parts that were more durable than human tissue. Or imagine some other kinds of problems. What if people no longer needed to go out-of-doors but could remain in a controlled atmosphere? What if people had contact lenses that allowed them to switch easily from telescopic to microscopic vision? What if people were no longer dependent on natural food? What if they learned to read each other's mind? Your solution should be one that's not possible now but might be in the future when science and technology have made further advances.

Once you've chosen your problem and have imagined a future solution for it, then start thinking about the different ways the solution might affect people, what kinds of reactions people might have to it. This will help you find a situation that you can build a story on. Notice that Asimov chooses the people most likely to be affected by teaching machines—schoolchildren. Then he tells a story about what happens when two children who have known only individual instruction from a computer find an old-fashioned book that tells them about the way school used to be.

You will find that when you're writing science fiction, your choice of point of view may be crucial. If you tell your story from the point of view of a scientist, you will have to make your readers believe that the scientist is real. This means putting in some scientific information—perhaps a lot of it. On the other hand, if you tell your story from the point of view of a nonscientist, then you don't need as much scientific detail.

Asimov tells his story from the point of view not of the County Inspector but of a child, Margie. That way he doesn't have to explain anything more about the mechanical teacher than a child would naturally observe. He doesn't even say it's a computer. From Margie's point of view it's "large and black and ugly." It has a screen and a slot for assignments and tests, and it requires her to write her answers in a punch code.

Telling your science-fiction story from the point of view of someone who doesn't know a great deal about science can help you cover up your own ignorance. You can save time that you might otherwise have to spend in research.

But there's another advantage—a more important one. Why did

Isaac Asimov, a very well-informed science writer as well as a creator of science fiction, choose to tell his story from a child's point of view? He didn't need to cover up his ignorance. The other advantage is this: You will be able to keep the scientific detail in your story to a minimum. Why is that an advantage? If you write your story from a scientifically knowledgeable point of view, you are likely to clutter it up with detail. You may have so much that your story could get almost unreadable. You'd be tempted to put in information for information's sake, not because it was important to the story.

Too much information is rather deadening.
—Willa Cather

Your science-fiction story will probably end up making a comment about how the future you have imagined compares with the present. Things may have become better, or they may have gotten worse. Asimov's story makes this comment about the future: If the teaching of the future is done by machines placed in pupils' houses, pupils may have the advantage of learning at their own pace. But to have no more human interaction between teacher and student and among students learning together would be a loss.

7. AN ALTERNATIVE TO FICTION

a nonfiction approach

Maybe you want to write something. But you don't particularly want to write a poem or a short story or a play. You'd rather write more directly about something that really happened. Why is that? Maybe it has occurred to you that there are things going on all the time in real life that are as fascinating as anything in fiction. Certain scenes in courtrooms and restaurants, on the street, around committee tables, backstage at the theater or the concert hall, in your own home. Some scenes are funny, not because a writer set them up that way, but because they are just naturally funny. Some are moments of crisis or change in people's lives. Such moments even seem to build toward a climax and to have the beginning-middle-ending structure that fiction has. Others are fascinating simply because they let you know what people are really like.

You get the feeling that if you could just describe the people and where they are and what they're doing, take down what they say, maybe leave out something here and there, you'd have it—a short story, but one that actually happened.

This shouldn't be surprising. After all, fiction writers base their stories on what goes on in real life—at least indirectly. They knock themselves out inventing "realistic" dialogue. They collect details from real life to make their characters more vivid. So why not reverse the process? Why not write up reality as if it were fiction? You won't invent the material—the setting, the characters, the events. You want your story to be factually accurate. You'll even use the real names of people and places. But you can use the techniques you've learned for writing fiction to present the material. You can use scenes with action and dialogue. You can use descriptive details that reveal personalities and life-styles. You can show people's thoughts and feelings.

What's more, you'll be trying out a form that professional writers have been experimenting with since the 1960s. It's called New Journalism. *Journalism* because it's used mostly for magazine articles. *New* because it wasn't until well into the 1960s that people started realizing that a handful of younger journalists and some novelists, too, were doing something different. They were writing nonfiction that sounded like fiction.

journalism, old and new

Until these New Journalists came along, magazine writers followed a pretty standard formula, especially in writing about people. According to the formula, you began your article with a snappy quotation. This led your readers to a statement of the main idea. Then you developed this idea through explanation and illustrated it with anecdotes and quotations. You saved one quotation for the end, one that sounded final, funny, or added an unexpected detail. Here's an example of the old-style journalism. It's the ending of a profile of Woody Allen.

> "If people come away relating to me as a person," Allen says, "rather than just enjoying my jokes, if they come away wanting to hear me again, no matter what I might talk about, then I'm succeeding." Judging by the returns, he is. Woody Allen is Mr. Related-To, Mr. Pop Therapy, of the mid-1960s, and he seems a good bet to hold the franchise for many years.
>
> Yet he does have a problem all his own, unshared by, unrelated to, the rest of America. "I'm obsessed," he says, "by the fact that my mother genuinely resembles Groucho Marx."   *—William Zinsser*

187

It's clear, just from the ending of this profile, that the writer is keeping an emotional distance between his subject and the readers. His goal is to explain why Woody Allen is popular. The Woody Allen in this excerpt is the same Woody Allen you'd see on film or on the stage. Zinsser is giving you, once again, the performer, the comedian with the oddball wisecrack up his sleeve. And that's all. That can be pretty entertaining, but it's old-style journalism.

The New Journalist is after something different. The New Journalist wants to show you what the subject is really like, below the surface, the way a novelist would reveal a character.

Here, in contrast to Zinsser's profile, is the beginning of a New Journalism article Jimmy Breslin wrote about the trial of a union official:

> It did not seem like a bad morning at all. The boss, Tony Provenzano, who is one of the biggest men in the Teamsters Union, walked up and down the corridor outside of this Federal courtroom in Newark and he had a little smile on his face and he kept flicking a white cigarette holder around.
>
> "Today is the kind of a day for fishing," Tony was saying. "We ought to go out and get some fluke."
>
> Then he spread his legs a little and went at this big guy named Jack, who had on a gray suit. Tony stuck out his left hand so he could throw a hook at this guy Jack. The big diamond ring on Tony's pinky flashed in the light coming through the tall windows of the corridor. Then Tony shifted and hit Jack with a right hand on the shoulder.
>
> "Always the shoulder," one of the guys in the corridor laughed. "Tony is always banging Jack on the shoulder."

It reads like fiction, but nothing is invented. Breslin has simply written down in the form of a scene what he actually observed. Breslin continues his article by shifting his scene from the corridor into the courtroom. He never stops to *explain* anything about Provenzano. Instead, he shows the sweat breaking out on Provenzano's upper lip when the judge starts lecturing him. And when Provenzano is sentenced to seven years in prison, Breslin shows

188

him twisting the diamond ring on his little finger. Breslin finishes
the article off with a scene in the courthouse cafeteria. He shows
you the young prosecutor on the case eating fried scallops and fruit
salad from a tray.

> Nothing on his hand flashed. The guy who sank Tony
> Pro doesn't even have a diamond ring on his pinky.

An old-style journalist wouldn't bother with such details. The old-
style journalist simply wants to tell you what happened. But Jimmy
Breslin wants to show you what people are really like. So he sifts
through the details of real events and recreates them as scenes.
This is the basic technique of the New Journalism.

the power of description

In a way the New Journalists have rediscovered the power of surface detail to reveal what people are like inside. At least they rely
on description far more than do most of today's fiction writers.

They fill their scenes with details of people's clothing and furniture, of their everyday gestures, poses, glances, habits, and manners, of their styles of eating, keeping house, traveling, working.

> **The recording of such details is not mere embroidery in prose. It lies as close to the center of the power of realism as any other device in literature.**
> **—Tom Wolfe**

Here's part of a New Journalism article about the movie actress Viva, who starred in several of the late Andy Warhol's experimental movies in the 1960s and 1970s. Notice how much you learn about her.

> On the third ring Viva opened the door to her East 83rd Street brownstone floor-through apartment. The young woman who stood at the door wore no make-up and her eyes were a spot of intense green color in a face of light brows and invisible eyelashes. She wore red slacks and [a] . . . red cotton blouse. Her hair was pulled back in a bun. As soon as I entered words started spilling out, "Oh . . . don't look at this place. I haven't cleaned up or picked up a thing in months. Every night I think I'll die from the smell of dust and that cockroach powder. Just look at those filthy windows. I've got to do

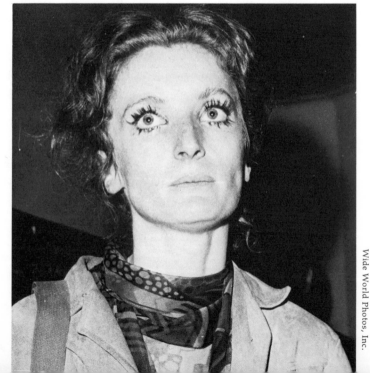

something about this, but I don't own a vacuum and I can't buy one. I'm penniless, absolutely penniless. . . ."

Viva stepped gracefully over underwear, dresses, bags of laundry, an iron, some dishes, magazines and papers. She leaned down and from under a laundry bag extracted the velvet coat I had seen her wearing the night before. It was badly burned. "Look at this—ruined. And all the hours I spent on airplanes sewing that lining. Someone dropped a lighted match on it and I didn't notice until it was all burned up. . . . It was my favorite. The only other dress I like is a 1920s dress Andy bought but it smells so of perspiration that I can't wear it. Oh, who cares," said Viva, walking through the stuffing that was oozing out of a gold chair and past a wall full of scrawled telephone numbers.

Viva led the way back into the bedroom. It contained a sheetless double bed which occupied almost the entire room. On it lay the remains of pancakes in a tinfoil dish, an orange juice container, some sweaters, a make-up mirror, various types of make-up, a copy of *The Little Prince* and some photographs. She scooped up the photographs. "I got these for you to see. They are of my family."
—*Barbara L. Goldsmith*

In this excerpt Barbara Goldsmith gives the impression of simply jotting down whatever she has observed. It's as if she were photographing the scene. Her description seems very natural and easy and casual. But, in fact, she has worked hard to choose only details that reveal the personality of her subject. Note, for example, the contrast she draws between the "gracefully" stepping Viva and the disorder of her apartment.

Selecting significant details is a harder job for the journalist than for the fiction writer. That's because the journalist starts from outside. Fiction writers can decide on a character trait and then think up details that will reveal that trait. But as a journalist, you can't work that way. First, you observe details. Then you have to decide what the details reveal, if anything. You need to be careful to choose only details that actually reveal something. If you choose them well enough, descriptive details can make your readers feel they know the people you're writing about inside and out.

WRITING NONFICTION SCENES

Here's a student-written article for you to read and experiment with. Though interesting, it is not in the style of the New Journalists. Try rewriting it in that style. But first, think in terms of scenes. How many scenes would you divide this material into? Two? Three? What would they be? Then, try writing a new beginning for the article. You might begin with a description or some dialogue. The object is to try to make the readers feel that they are there, watching what's happening.

There will be parts of this article that you won't be able to use. Be ready to discuss in class which ones they are and why you can't use them. You'll also discover that it would be easier to transform this article into New Journalism if you had more details to work with. For instance, the writer says, "Mr. Stewart also displayed a ready humor." Wouldn't a New Journalist use a quotation here instead of a summary? Again, take this statement, "Mr. Stewart's daughter had prepared a wonderful dinner for all of us." Wouldn't a New Journalist describe the meal? Maybe write: "We ate thick slabs of smoked ham that she had fried in coffee in an iron pan"? Prepare a list of the kinds of details that you feel would make the article more vivid and easier to recreate in scenes. Be ready to discuss your list in class.

> Many years ago [people] . . . who worked skillfully with wood were indispensable to those around them. Everything from houses to banjos required wood, and [people] . . . who knew how to work with wood were needed in every community. One essential trade was that of a cooper—someone who made kegs, barrels, buckets, and other related vessels. These wooden containers were used to hold cornmeal, water, salted meat, nails—anything that could be stored or carried in them.
>
> We at *Foxfire* had been interested for a long time in finding a master of this trade, but could not locate anyone who was still actively working at it. Finally, Mr. Bill Henry, a member of the Southern Highlands Handicraft Guild and one of our subscribers, told us of a friend of his in Sneedville, Tennessee who was still making churns, buckets, and large wooden tubs. He offered to direct us

there and introduce us, and we gratefully accepted. Four of our staff members went to Sneedville and ended up spending an entire day with Alex Stewart—watching, listening, and recording as he made a churn. We found him to be one of the most interesting men we have ever met.

Born and reared on Newman Ridge within sight of his present home, Mr. Stewart grew up watching and learning from his father and grandfather, both of whom had worked with wood all their lives. From them he learned to cut and season his own wood and make all his own tools by hand. The outbuildings on his farm include a small sawmill and a blacksmith shop where he forges the tools he works with. He has power tools as well, but he prefers his own handmade manual and foot-powered tools, feeling that he has better control with them and gets the job done just as quickly.

In the course of the day we spent with Mr. Stewart, we were not only impressed with his work, but with the things he said. He readily answered all our questions and often made interesting comments of his own.

"I've made all my tools, matter a'fact, ever'thing I got. Well, this [shaving horse, a kind of workbench] I guess is about fifty years old. I used t'have another'un. It got old, an' I made this'un. If I've got it right, this is th'second one there is in the United States made like this. They's one more like it, and I made it. My grandfather, I learnt this from him. He made ever'thing—wheels, anything could be thought about, he made it, an' I got th'pattern off'a his'n. An' m'daddy—he worked at it as long as he lived. I've been doin' it since I'uz old enough t'do it . . . about sixty-five or seventy years. When I'uz young, ever'time I'd get a chance, I'uz a'foolin' with it. Yeah, I just delighted in it. Anything that you delight in, it ain't any trouble for you t'do it, but somethin' you don't delight in, it's pretty hard.

"Yeah, I made these tools. I used t'make about anything I wanted to. It's a lot better than stuff you buy. It makes me feel good. I've made many of a churn an' sold

it for two dollars. No, not a regret, not in this line [of work]."

Mr. Stewart also displayed a ready humor and often had us smiling or laughing as he worked and talked. One of the most pleasant and touching surprises we had that day occurred at noon when we discovered Mr. Stewart's daughter had prepared a wonderful dinner for all of us. The large table fairly groaned under the weight of all the good food. We ate an incredible amount and then trooped back out to continue our work, well satisfied.

A description of Alex Stewart would not be complete without telling about the workshop where he spends so much time. It is located in the barn which stands behind and to the left of his house. Probably the first thing one notices in walking into the barn is the sight and smell of cedar, stacked in the corner to dry, and lying all over the floor in the form of chips and shavings. Mr. Stewart uses cedar to make his churns, buckets, and other containers because cedar doesn't shrink when drying out after it has been wet. Some people use poplar as it is always easy to work with, but it is apt to shrink after it has been wet if water is not left in it.

On the right-hand wall hang the handmade tools. In their respective places stand the handmade shaving horse, foot-powered lathe, and jointer. Also scattered about are various things he has made—churns, barrels, buckets, piggins, and a big, wooden washtub. It was here that we discovered that he also makes rolling pins, bread boards, brooms, ingenious little wooden puzzles, and many other things. His son, Milum, showed us many of these things and told us about them.

Alex Stewart did indeed become a person for whom we developed a vast amount of respect and admiration as we watched and listened to him, and at the end of the day, when we were forced to say good-bye and head back, we all agreed that we came away with much more than the directions for . . . [making a churn].   —*Laurie Brunson*

one on one

Let's say you'd like to write an article in the style of the New Journalists. You'd like to use the techniques of fiction to make a real story vivid. Maybe you'd like to do an interview. What kind of person would make the best subject? You might be tempted to say, "Somebody very important or famous, the head of a giant corporation, an astronaut, a TV star." The truth is that interviews with well-known people are often dull. And that's because when you meet them, they're usually not doing whatever it is that made them famous or important. Instead of clumping across the surface of the moon, they're there at the airport, between planes, answering the same stale questions they've answered before.

New Journalists don't bother much with press conferences. They haven't found them very good places to learn about people. When they write about celebrities, the New Journalists show them coping with the irritations of daily routine, rehearsing something over and over, dealing with other people, throwing tantrums, acting like phonies. But celebrities aren't the only interesting people around. Some interesting people are found at the edge of important events —the surgeon who tried to save John Kennedy's life, the man who dug his grave. Others may be interesting because of their attitude toward their work—the obituary writer for *The New York*

Times, a professional dog walker. And it's not the kind of job, necessarily, that creates the interest. It's how the person and the job are described. On the face of it, you'd probably say that hiking cars is a pretty uninteresting way to make a living. But there's an art to being a good car hiker. There's an art to finding parking spaces on crowded city streets when no one else can. A New Journalist shows you that art in this excerpt:

> Without saying a word, Roy bolts from my side and sprints 40 yards up his tree-lined block, . . . jumps in a car and revs it up.
>
> Roy has seen what I had not; a man in one of those $42 East Side Bohemian bulky-knit sweaters is leading his two children toward his Pontiac; now he is opening the front door for them. There is a motion picture theater nearby; cars are coursing through the block, Roy roars up in his M.D. floater, a black Ford Galaxie, and stops right alongside the Pontiac. [A doctor, with . . . (an) M.D. license plate, is the most sought-after client in the whole East Side doorman-parking operation. The doorman can stash the M.D. cars in no parking spaces while he shifts other cars around.]
>
> The man in the sweater looks out, nonplussed, but Roy motions him to go ahead and start pulling out. Roy backs

Laurence Risser

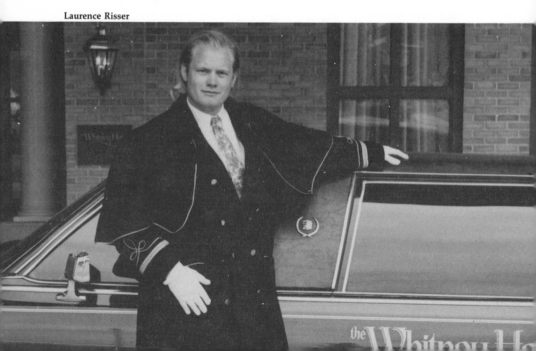

up slowly to give him room. A man in a Rambler sees the Pontiac is getting ready to pull out and pulls up ahead so he can back in. So Roy takes off his visor hat and moves up right behind him, blowing his horn. The Rambler takes off. Roy backs up again, just behind the Pontiac once more. A Ford from New Jersey with four kids in it, double-dating, pulls up ahead to back in. Roy puts his visor hat back on, roars up behind it, blows the horn, chases it off, then backs up again as the Pontiac leaves the curb. Roy whips in there and the space is saved. Two spaces, actually.

Roy bounds back in front of the door.

"See how I parked it?" he says. "It takes up two spaces. That's what you've got to do when you have too many vacant spaces. You stretch 'em. You have to move all these cars back and forth like an accordion. You can always spot a set-up like this. On an ordinary street the cars are all crammed up. Here they're stretched out. See these keys"—he pulled a vast ring out from under the frogging of his uniform—"a duplicate for every regular. You couldn't run this thing without 'em. . . .

"I'll tell you something else. You have to know *people.* When a guy brings his kid out to the car, he's not just going to reach inside and get something out of the glove compartment. He's *leaving.* That's the time you have to run for the floater.

"Also you notice how I blocked off that spot. You can't pull up *ahead* of somebody pulling out, because one of these Volkswagens or something—boy, you ask any doorman, they *hate* these Volkswagens—they'll pull right in there while you're up ahead with your chin hanging.

"And did you notice this business I do with the hats? This, if you don't mind me saying it, is finesse. If you want to chase off an older guy—you know, an adult—you take the hat off, because an older guy, he'll see this doorman trying to bluff him out of the spot, and he'll say to himself, 'Well, that clown isn't shoving me around, I'm not ninety-seven years old for nothing.' But for the kids, you put the hat *on.* A kid in a car, he feels guilty a little,

197

you know, even if he hasn't done anything. Don't ask me why, but it's true. So he sees this hat, and even if he knows it isn't a cop, he's not sure what it is, you know? So he scrams off. You saw how that kid scrammed off? That's what I mean, you have to know *people*."

—*Tom Wolfe*

The point isn't that car hikers make better subjects than astronauts or tycoons or TV stars. The point is that you can write an interesting article if you observe your subject at work and if you're alert to the scene taking place before your eyes. That's what counts in New Journalism, not a fistful of prepared questions. If you want to ask questions after the scene is over—fine. But don't start off, "Can you tell me any interesting experiences you've had on the job?" That's old-style journalism. And it just won't yield the same results.

> **You try not to get in the way of the person you're trying to show. . . . You're trying to follow . . . the person . . . instead of coming . . . with a lot of prepared questions.   —Lillian Ross**

Alertness to the scene also means being alive to details that might not strike you at first as part of the scene. For instance, interruptions. Notice how Barbara Goldsmith makes use of the telephone call that interrupted her interview with Viva.

> The phone rang. Viva picked it up and said, "O.K., O.K., I've put the check in the mail. You can't cut off my electricity. I told you, I've been away. It's all taken care of." She hung up and said, "I've got to call Andy to pay my Con Edison bill. . . . We're all supposed to go on regular salary soon, but Andy says the company is bankrupt."   —*Barbara L. Goldsmith*

Viva's breezy handling of the utility company is very revealing. It suggests that she has a live-for-the-day attitude. So, when you're interviewing, if the phone rings, friends or co-workers arrive on the scene, your subject's kids come trouping in, or even if someone turns up selling vacuum cleaners, keep listening and watching. These details may add realism to your article. They may even give you additional insight into the personality of your subject.

REPORTING ON ACTION

Find a person in your community with a job that might make interesting material for a New Journalism article. Make arrangements for on-the-scene observation. You could go along on a commercial fishing boat. Ride along with a garbage truck. Get a haircut and stay to observe the scene. Ride along with a tow truck that helps stranded motorists. Show up at a construction site. Accompany a real estate agent who's showing houses. Spend the day with someone in the customer service department of a department store. Observe a typesetter at a newspaper publisher, or a traffic-court judge. Observe a store clerk dealing with customers.

Try to collect enough material—descriptive details of appearance, clothing, mannerisms, movements, surroundings, and talk—to write at least one scene. Even if you aren't entirely sure what's going on, don't interrupt the flow of the scene to ask questions. Wait until afterward.

PLANNING WHAT TO INCLUDE

Once in a while, the details leading up to an interview are as revealing as anything the subject does or says. Read the following excerpt from an article written by Joan Didion. What does the material tell you about Joan Baez, a folksinger and activist prominent in the late '60s and '70s?

> It is difficult to arrange to see Joan Baez, at least for anyone not tuned to the underground circuits of the protest movement. The New York company for which she records, Vanguard, will give only Manny Greenhill's number, in Boston. "Try Area Code 415, prefix DA 4, number 4321," Manny Greenhill [her manager] will rasp. Area Code 415, DA 4-4321 will connect the caller with Keppler's Bookstore in Palo Alto [California], which is where Ira Sandperel [president of Miss Baez's Institute for the Study of Nonviolence] used to work. Someone at the bookstore will take a number, and, after checking with Carmel to see if anyone there cares to hear from the

caller, will call back, disclosing a Carmel number. The
Carmel number is not, as one might think by now, for
Miss Baez, but for an answering service. The service will
take a number, and, after some days or weeks, a call may
or may not be received from Judy Flynn, Miss Baez's
secretary. Miss Flynn says that she will "try to contact"
Miss Baez. "I don't see people," says the heart of this
curiously improvised web of wrong numbers, disconnected
telephones, and unreturned calls. "I lock the gate and
hope nobody comes, but they come anyway. Somebody's
been telling them where I live."

going inside

Probably most New Journalists rely on surface detail and quotation to show what people are like. But some also use the fictional
technique of the omniscient narrator. They try to present an event

as it's being experienced by the person they're writing about. They do this by revealing the person's thoughts and feelings.

> I try to write . . . [the scene] from the point of view of the persons I am writing about, even revealing whenever possible what these individuals are thinking during those moments that I am describing.
>
> —Gay Talese

Here's part of a newspaper article in which the writer uses the technique of the omniscient narrator:

Jane Lynch stared down at the white goose-quill pens, neatly crossed, on the highly polished mahogany table. Though she appeared poised, her heart was doing funny things. The pens harkened back to John Quincy Adams, Daniel Webster, and Henry Clay, traditionally provided should attorneys wish to make notes. Jane Lynch, 27, was not yet a lawyer. But sitting beside her, her teacher, De Paul University law professor Patrick Keenan, nodded reassuringly, and studied his own notes.

Lynch stole a quick glance at the high bench before her—two massive wings angled inward at 18 degrees so the justices could watch and avoid interrupting each other. Jane wished Justice William O. Douglas was going to be there. He always dozed during oral arguments, but she knew he would have been on her side. Douglas, though, was ill and was expected to retire.

Behind Lynch, in the hall of the great chamber, other De Paul law students shared her emotions that morning last December. It was impossible not to be impressed . . . The chamber's motif of bone white and veined marble, offset by heavy red-velvet draperies and dark upholstery, imparts a majesty even young children sense. They sit quietly without being told.

Lynch gathered her thoughts and her papers as the hall hushed. At precisely 10 a.m., the crier crashed his gavel. "The honorable, the chief justice and the associate justices of the Supreme Court of the United States," he intoned, as the black-robed jurists briskly stepped through openings in the curtain.

Lynch forgot her nerves and prepared to assist Keenan as he argued her brief against the State of Illinois in behalf of Timmy Robertson and 15,000 other foster children. "Mr. Chief Justice," Keenan began, "and may it please the court . . ." —*Peter Gorner*

You may say that showing what Jane Lynch thought and felt isn't journalism at all. It's pure fiction. How can anyone know for sure what's going on in another person's mind? The answer is, You ask. Not, of course, while the action is going on, but afterward. Then you say, "When you were sitting there, waiting for the justices to come in, what was running through your mind?" But

202

you don't use what the person tells you as a quotation. Instead, you rewrite it and work it into your narrative. For instance, Jane Lynch may have told the journalist, "I felt nervous but kind of excited." In the article this shows up as "her heart was doing funny things."

DESCRIBING WHAT YOU FEEL

Before you write about someone else's thoughts and feelings, why not try bringing readers into your own mind? Make yourself the main character in the scene you're recreating. New Journalists frequently do this. Here's the idea: By showing how you felt during an experience, you can bring your readers closer to that experience, maybe closer than they might ever be able to get by themselves. Skydiving, for instance. Lots of people are curious about how it feels to take that jump out of the plane into the cold air, wondering if the parachute will open. But how many ever get around to trying it for themselves? Here's one who did, Gloria Emerson:

> He took me to the doorway, sat me down, and yelled "Go!" or "Now!" or "Out!" There was nothing to do but be punched by the wind, which knocked the spit from my mouth, reach for the wing strut, hold on hard, kick back the feet so weighted and helpless in those boots, and let go. The parachute opened with a plop, as Istel had sworn to me that it would. When my eyelids opened as well, I saw the white gloves on my hands were old ones from Saks Fifth Avenue, gloves I wore with summer dresses. There was dribble on my chin; my eyes and nose were leaking. I wiped everything with the gloves.
>
> There was no noise; the racket of the plane and wind had gone away. The cold and sweet stillness seemed an astonishing, undreamed-of gift. Then I saw what I had never seen before, will never see again: endless sky and earth in colors and textures no one had ever described. Only then did the parachute become a most lovable and docile toy: this wooden knob to go left, this wooden knob to go right. The pleasure of being there, the drifting and the calm, rose to a fever; I wanted to stay pinned in the air and stop the ground from coming closer. The target

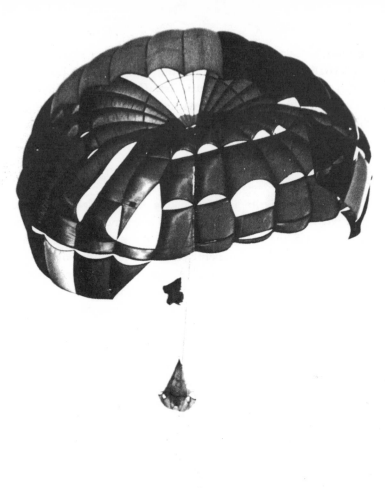

was a huge arrow in a sandpit. I was cross to see it, afraid
of nothing now, for even the wind was kind and the
trees looked soft. I landed on my feet in the pit with a
bump, then sat down for a bit.

Here Gloria Emerson lets readers share in her first plunge
from a plane. She makes the experience vivid by writing

down everything she felt from the moment she went through the hatch until she hit the ground. She includes physical sensations, emotions, random thoughts—everything that was part of the experience.

Do you have to jump out of a plane to find something unusual to write about? Not really. You can make anything unusual by the way you write about it. That's because everybody reacts differently to experiences. But write about something you're about to do for the first time. That way the experience will make a stronger impression on you.

Suppose you're about to take your first "solo" in the family car. Pay attention to what you're going through. Keep track of everything that strikes you: How small the rearview mirror seems. How many different arrangements of tail lights there are. How some drivers just can't drive for even a block without using their horns. Will you make it through the intersection before the child hesitating on the corner dashes out? What if that big black Buick on the left fails to yield? Then write it all down right away while all the sights, sounds, smells, textures, hopes, fears, discoveries are still sharp in your memory. That way you'll make your readers feel they are sharing your experience. Your point of view will make the experience unique.

The important thing is not to be vague. So don't try to write about something that happened in the past, even the recent past. It won't be strong enough in your memory to make good New Journalism. Instead, plan to write up an experience you're about to have. And while you're going through the experience, don't forget for a moment that you are a writer who must communicate that experience to others.

group portrait

Maybe it seems strange, but even groups have personalities. A bunch of people can act like one person—all of them angry, mean, worried, happy, or silly. Or they can have such different and even conflicting attitudes that you wonder how they even think of themselves as a group.

Gloria Emerson

Jimmy Breslin

Tom Wolfe

Joan Didion

Barbara Goldsmith

Farrar, Straus and Giroux
Photo by Julian Wasser

Farrar, Straus and Giroux
Photo by Frank Perry

rar, Straus and Giroux
oto by Dennis Shattuck

New Journalists are always on the lookout for groups of all kinds. They know that any time people get together and start talking, there's bound to be some kind of drama, some interplay of personalities.

New Journalists also know, as fiction writers have long known, that nothing involves readers more completely than realistic dialogue. That's because dialogue can reveal the different personalities of several people more quickly and effectively than any other device. So when they write about groups, New Journalists fill their scenes with dialogue, sometimes long stretches of it. Sometimes they even write articles that are made up almost completely of dialogue. In these they don't give an interpretation of what's going on. They just let people reveal themselves through what they say. It's up to the readers to draw their own conclusions, to decide what the journalist was trying to show.

Here's a New Journalist's account of a meeting. Instead of making a flat statement, "A group of experts can sometimes look pretty silly," she shows them fumbling around, trying to deal with a simple question.

"But what can we say music is, then?" asked the woman in the second row.

It was Saturday afternoon in Newberry Library.

Composers Lejaren Hiller of the University of Illinois and Ramon Zupko of Roosevelt University had spoken to the members of the International Society for Contemporary Music, Chicago Chapter. The topic: the new music in Poland.

Tapes of short works by composers Lutoslawski and Penderecki had been played. The panel moderator, music critic Bernard Jacobson, had just opened the discussion.

"We've always said that music is organized sound. Harmony, melody, rhythm. But now what do we say? That it's organized noise?" The woman looked concerned.

"Noise is something that interferes—as, for example, static on the telephone," began Zupko.

"Noise is the part of the signal that is not the message," said the man in charge of the tape recorder.

"In my music, I like to use the sound of a body falling down the stairs," contributed Hiller.

"But harmony, melody, rhythm—what can we tell children that music is?" the woman wanted to know. "Should we say that it's organized noise?"

"I should think that if we defer to the scientific method —at least insofar as I am acquainted with the philosophy of science—we will find that definitions are not fruitful. It's not a matter of saying that music must be this or that but of pointing to a particular musical work and saying, 'I think this is a good work because it has certain characteristics,'" said Jacobson.

"Then we can conclude that music is organized noise." The woman seemed in some way satisfied.

"What exactly has been the impact of John Cage in the new music of Poland?" asked a young man.

"Oh, very considerable," said Hiller. "During the Warsaw Festival, a composer actually jumped off the platform and did karate rolls down the aisle."

"Why was that necessary?" asked another man, as if he expected an answer.

"Is Cage one of the great ones?" asked a woman.

Zupko smiled. "Well, of course, his philosophy has been more significant than his music."

"He introduced the idea of concert theatrics," added Hiller, "which many composers are taking up."

"Is there anything in this new Polish music that is nationalistic?" came another query. "You know, on the radio, every time they want to introduce Poland, they play the Chopin Polonaise."

Hiller: "I think we could say that the Polish music tends to be dramatic, flamboyant, while the new German music is more somber."

Zupko handed around several beautifully drawn graph scores. They featured such innovations as one inch on the paper equaling one second in musical time. "As you can see," he said, "there is also a fascination with graphics as such. It was said of one composer that his music isn't performed much, but he has regular exhibitions of his scores."

—*Anita Klemsrud*

Notice how clear a view Anita Klemsrud gives you of each person by the way she selects dialogue. It's as if she moves a spotlight from person to person, revealing each one. There's the persistent woman with her simple but difficult question. There's the tape operator who thinks in the jargon of a sound engineer. There are the two composers: One is happy about the theatrical trends in new music and eager to show that his own music is right up to the minute. The other is quick to point out other composers' weaknesses. Then there's the music critic who's stuffy and long-winded.

The idea is to create the impression that the dialogue is being recorded in full. This is, of course, only an illusion. If you tried to use all the talk you heard in a scene you were recreating, you'd have more than you could handle. And a lot of it would be boring, too.

So you need to select your talk carefully. Test it by the same standards you use when you invent dialogue for fiction. Ask yourself, Does it reveal the person who is speaking? Is it interesting? Is it well paced? It may be real, but does it sound natural?

You also need to select talk carefully so that your scene makes a point. Notice that Klemsrud shows the lack of coherence in the meeting without making her article incoherent.

You will probably have to improve most talk before you can use it as dialogue. The question is, How far can you go? As long as you don't distort the meaning of what someone has said, you can do quite a bit. You can prune individual speeches, making them shorter, tightening up their structure. You can combine parts of several speeches by one person. You can even change the order of speaking, to make the dialogue clearer or more interesting. But don't make up statements just so the dialogue will flow more smoothly or because you can think of something a little more clever to say. Leave invention for the fiction writer.

GETTING A TALK STORY

Attend a meeting of some organization that you think would make a good talk story. Go to a meeting of a citizens group

—the Committee for Saving the Trees, Citizens Concerned about Old Buildings, senior citizens. Or a professional meeting—a union meeting, a professional convention in a hotel, a meeting of the Business and Professional Women's Club. Or even a community government session—City Council, Park and Recreation Board. Sit in on a rehearsal—community theater, children's pageant, opera society, orchestra, chamber group, rock group. Try listening to talk in waiting rooms—in an airport, a bus depot, a doctor's office. Go to a sports event and listen to the people in the crowd instead of watching the game. Listen to the conversation at a party. Ride back and forth on a subway or a bus and keep track of the talk. Listen to a radio talk show.

Start taking notes on any talk you hear right away. You don't know just when or how a little drama might begin. You may need some of the earlier routine talk to provide a framework for your scene or to show the personalities of the speakers.

What about using a tape recorder? You could record conversation, but most New Journalists don't. There's a psychological reason. People tend to freeze when they know they're being recorded. Also, recording is impractical. You may get miles of talk on tape that you'll have to spend hours transcribing. It's better to train yourself to take good notes and to write up the scene as soon as you can after you've observed it.

Select dialogue that reveals the different personalities in the group you're writing about. Include any summary you need to make the situation clear. Because you are writing journalism, you still need to get the basic facts—who, what, when, where—into your article somewhere. Try to arrange talk, summary, and description in such a way that you create a scene with a point. Your talk story should be a group portrait. It should reveal something about the group.

8. MAKING IT PUBLIC

how to prepare your manuscript

Your story, poem, play, article is written. You've revised it and polished it, and you're satisfied that it says just what you want it to say. But now what do you do with it? You probably want to find out how readers will react to what you've written. You want to know if you're really communicating. If you tuck your story or poem away in your desk drawer, you may never know what you've accomplished. Instead, you should try to find some way of publishing what you've written.

The trial by market everything must come to.
—Robert Frost

The first step toward publication is to type your manuscript in publishable form using a typewriter or, if you have a personal computer, a word-processing program.

The way your manuscript is typed tells a lot about you as a writer. If it's sloppy, with uneven margins, single-spaced lines, or pages of different lengths, it'll be immediately obvious that you're an amateur. What's worse, it will give the impression that you don't care about what you've written. An editor, looking at a poorly prepared manuscript, might reason: If the writer doesn't care enough to provide a neat manuscript, why should anyone else take it seriously? An editor will delay reading a manuscript that's messy and hard to read, delay perhaps forever. So make the editor's job as easy as you can. It's a simple courtesy. And while it won't necessarily get your manuscript published, it will at least get it read.

The procedures that professionals follow in preparing manuscripts are simple. Once you're acquainted with them, they'll become automatic.

Type or print out your manuscript on white paper, 8½ by 11 inches. Use good-quality paper, not thin tissue. Don't use the kind of paper called erasable. The type on this kind of paper often blurs and even rubs off with handling. And a manuscript goes through many hands in the process of being published.

214

Make sure your typewriter or printer has a ribbon fresh enough to leave a sharp, black imprint on the paper. Avoid colored ribbons, even blue ones.

Set your margins to allow 1½ inches of space on the left and about an inch on the right. Top and bottom margins should each be 1½ inches. The reason for fairly wide margins is that editors need space to put in instructions for the typesetter.

On the first page, type your name and address in the upper left-hand corner, single-spaced. If you're typing a short story or an article, then about halfway down the first page type the title, centered on the page, in capital letters. One line under the title, a little to the right, type your by-line. Triple-space between your by-line and the first line of copy. After that, double-space. Indent paragraphs five spaces. Your first page should look like this:

```
Alison Brookston
1314 West Oak Street
De Kalb, IL 60115
```

```
                    ROLES
                by Alison Brookston

     Jane was sick and tired of having to defend herself.

She wanted to be a pilot; that was that.

     As she picked up this month's issue of Flying from

the library shelf, she could hear Tim chuckling behind

her. She looked over at the corner table where he was

sitting. He was grinning again. It made her mad. He

never came right out and made fun of her. But he got

that silly grin on his face every time she mentioned

wanting to be a pilot.

     She scowled at him and then sat down to read her

magazine. There was a 747 on the cover. What a beautiful

plane. She wondered how it would feel to command a plane
```

If you're typing a play manuscript, you have to observe a few special requirements. Put the names of the characters in capital letters. Indicate by underlining that stage directions are to be set in italic type. Type the first line of each speech even with the left-hand margin. Indent additional lines one space. The first page of your play manuscript should look like this:

```
        Mattie Saunders
        5551 South Dorchester Avenue
        Chicago, IL 60637




                        THE PHONE CALL
                        by Mattie Saunders

    Scene. LINDA'S bedroom.

    As the curtain opens, JILL is alone. She's standing in
    front of a full-length mirror, holding LINDA'S wedding
    dress in front of her. At the sound of a door closing
    offstage, JILL hastily hangs up the wedding dress. LINDA
    comes into the room, carrying the mail--a package and a
    number of letters and cards.
    JILL: Oh, Linda, it's you. I'm so excited. I've never
     been a maid of honor before.
    LINDA: (Casually glancing through the letters.) Then
     we're even, Jill. I've never been a bride before.
     (Continues reading.)
```

If you are typing a short poem or several poems, plan on one poem per page. Center the poem both vertically and horizontally on the page like this:

```
Ronald Selz
1000 Hammond Street
Los Angeles, CA 90069




                           LOVE
                        by Ronald Selz

        Let's sit for a while and simply talk

        Of you and me,

        Very softly, using

        Eyes as well as words.
```

You don't need to number the first page of a manuscript, but number each of the following pages in the upper right-hand corner. On those pages, type your last name in the upper left-hand corner as shown:

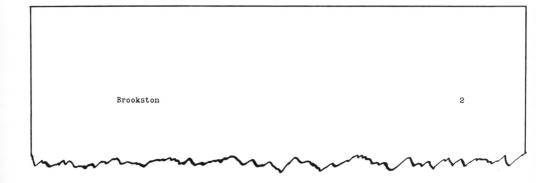

Brookston   2

That way, if a page becomes separated from the rest of the manuscript, it will be clear exactly where it belongs.

Type on one side of the paper only.

Proofread each page carefully before you take it out of the typewriter. Look for errors in spelling and punctuation as well as typing mistakes.

Don't forget to make at least one carbon or photocopy of your manuscript. Editors assume that you have your own copy on file. Manuscripts can and do get lost.

When you've completed typing the manuscript, you can fasten the pages with a paper clip. Don't staple them together or enclose them in a binder. Loose pages are easier for an editor to handle.

If your manuscript is short—fewer than five pages—you can fold it and mail it in a regular envelope for letters. If it's longer, mail it flat in a big manila envelope. Mark the envelope, Special Fourth Class Rate: Manuscript. That way, it won't cost you much to mail it. Check with the post office for the exact rate. Don't forget to include a self-addressed stamped envelope. It should be the same size as the envelope in which you submit your manuscript. Be sure it has enough postage to pay for the return of your manuscript if it is rejected. Otherwise, the manuscript will probably not be returned.

where to send it

It's not easy for beginning writers to get published. If you compete head-on with adult professionals, you'll probably end up with a collection of rejection slips.

Fortunately, there are a number of special opportunities for student writers. Some of these are writing contests that you may enter on your own. Others are competitions to which your creative writing teacher or other school representative may submit your writing for special recognition. These opportunities offer you a chance to see your work in print and sometimes to receive cash awards. Here are a few of the best-known competitions.

NCTE Achievement Awards in Writing
National Council of Teachers of English
1111 Kenyon Road
Urbana, IL 61801
Nominations of student work to be submitted by teachers before January 23. The Program to Recognize Excellence in Student Literary Magazines is also sponsored by the NCTE. The faculty advisor for your school's literary magazine may enter your school's magazine in this competition. July 1 is the deadline for submitting entries.

Poetry Society of America
15 Gramercy Park South
New York, NY 10003
Elias Lieberman Student Award of $100 for original, unpublished poems. Send for complete submission rules and requirements.

Scholastic Writing Awards
Scholastic Inc.
730 Broadway
New York, NY 10003
Annual writing competition for short stories, poems, essays, humor, and dramatic scripts. Submit in January.

Fiction Contest
Seventeen Magazine
850 Third Avenue
New York, NY 10022
See November issue of *Seventeen* for rules. *Seventeen* also publishes student writing (essays, poems, short stories, and articles) in the "Voices and Views" section of the magazine. Original manuscripts are

accepted for review throughout the year. Write to the Teen Feature editor at the above address, explaining your proposed topic and approach and requesting guidelines. To be considered, you must be under 21.

Teenage Fiction Contest
Teenage Magazine
217 Jackson Street
Box 948
Lowell, MA 01853
Short stories between 10-15 pages preferred. Submit to editorial office by February 1. Read *Teenage Magazine* for contest rules or send a self-addressed, stamped envelope for a copy.

Writer's Digest Writing Contest
Writers' Digest
9933 Alliance Road
Cincinnati, OH 45242
Annual contest for best short story, article, or poem. Submit by May 30. Not limited to students.

Check with your teacher to see if there is a special writing contest for high school students in your state or community. National writing opportunities and contests for high school students, like those previously listed, are compiled in the National Advisory List of Contests and Activities, distributed by the National Association of Secondary School Principals and available through your school office.

An excellent tool for young writers aspiring to be published is the *Market Guide for Young Writers,* written by Kathy Henderson and published by Shoe Tree Press, a division of Betterway Publications Inc. The 1988-1989 edition includes lists of writing contests and markets open to those under 21, and offers helpful advice.

If you decide to enter the professional marketplace, study the market first. Look for a magazine that publishes the sort of material you've written. A popular reference tool professional writers use for such research is the *Writer's Market,* which comes out annually. Before you mail your manuscript, send a letter or inquiry. Editors prefer to get letters of inquiry first. In it, explain as briefly as you can what you have written or are about to write and why it is suitable for that publication. Always include a self-addressed, stamped envelope with inquiries or submissions.

National Council of Teachers of English
1111 Kenyon Road, Urbana, Illinois 61801

Achievement Awards in Writing, 1989

Nominations must be sent to NCTE by January 23, 1989

The Entries:
Two Written Compositions

1. An impromptu theme written under teacher supervision in no more than 75 minutes and submitted in longhand without revision. The topic is designated by NCTE.

2. One sample of writing (prose **or** verse) that the student considers his or her best work, regardless of amount of revision. The "best writing" should not exceed ten typed, double-spaced pages. Research papers, term papers, or novels **will not** be accepted by state coordinators. Unlike the impromptu theme, the sample of best writing does not depend on information from NCTE. As soon as a student is nominated, therefore, he or she may begin work on the sample of best writing.

Nominees must submit both entries. The impromptu theme topic along with further instructions is sent in March to the teacher designated on the nomination blank. If the topic is not received by **April 1,** contact NCTE Achievement Awards. Both entries must be submitted to the state coordinator in one package, postmarked no later than April 21, 1989. Names and addresses of state coordinators are included in the instructions sent in March.

No entries are returned. Teachers or students should make copies of the compositions before submitting the originals. No publication of a student's work will be made without his or her prior written permission.

Judging of Entries

Teams of judges from the nominee's state, consisting of both high school and college English teachers, evaluate the entries for content and form. Each piece of writing is read by two judges. A state coordinator organizes the network of judges in each state and reports the results to NCTE.

1989 Schedule and Deadlines

January 23
Deadline for schools to return nomination blanks to NCTE, one blank for each nominee. **Only nomination blanks are to be submitted at this time, no compositions.** Nomination blanks postmarked after January 23, 1989, may be disqualified.

March
NCTE mails the impromptu theme topic and further instructions to the teachers specified on the nomination blanks.

April 21
Deadline for teachers to mail nominees' impromptu themes and samples of best writing to their state coordinators. Both compositions are to be sent in one package. Names and addresses of state coordinators are included with the instructions sent to teachers in March. These materials are **not** to be sent to NCTE.

August 1
State coordinators report results to NCTE.

October
NCTE announces the awards. Winners and their high school principals are notified by mail. Nominees who did not place in the competition are sent letters acknowledging their participation in the program.

Please note: teachers are not notified, only students.

Queries

Address queries to Achievement Awards in Writing, National Council of Teachers of English, 1111 Kenyon Road, Urbana, Illinois 61801.

The National Council of Teachers of English is happy to have the continuing support of both the New York Times Company Foundation and the Maurice R. Robinson Fund for the Achievement Awards in Writing. M. R. Robinson, founder of Scholastic Magazines, Inc., and longtime friend of NCTE, shared our concern for the importance of writing in a student's education. With the 1989 Achievement Awards, we are again calling to the attention of students an expanded audience for their writing through cooperation with the Scholastic Writing Awards. NCTE Achievement Award recipients will be offered the option of having what they selected as the sample of their best work submitted to the Scholastic Writing Awards. Nominees who are not award winners may enter their best work in the Scholastic program in the fall. Nominees interested in this opportunity should keep in mind the following Scholastic Writing Awards length requirements:

Short story—1,300 to 3,000 words

Short-short story—600 to 1,300 words

Poetry (single poem or group of poems)—50 to 200 lines

Essay—600 to 1,500 words

Humor—600 to 1,500 words

Dramatic script—not to exceed 30 minutes of performing time

For a full listing of categories and rules write for the Official Rules Booklet, Scholastic Writing Awards, 730 Broadway, New York, NY 10003.

SCHOLASTIC WRITING AWARDS

The nation's largest student writing program.

- Cash Awards • Scholarship Grants
- Other Prizes and National Honors

Open to students in grades 7 to 12 who may submit original

- short stories   • essays
- poems   • humor
      • dramatic scripts

Judged by distinguished panels of nationally-known authors, editors and educators.

Deadline for entries: Mid-January (See rules book for more information.)

For complete information and your official rules booklet write to:

Scholastic Writing Awards
730 Broadway
New York, NY 10003

**CONDUCTED BY
SCHOLASTIC INC.**

**CO-SPONSORED BY
SMITH CORONA AND APPLE COMPUTER**

The National Association of Secondary School Principals has placed this program on its approved Advisory List of National Contests and Activities.

creative writing club

You'll probably have to wait several weeks or even months for an editor's response to your manuscript. Even then, the response may be general and impersonal. You may want a more immediate, personal, and detailed reaction to what you've written. You'd like specific comments that will help you to develop as a writer. Your teacher can give you a detailed critique of your work. But you may also want to get comments from other student writers. You could form a creative writing club—call it a forum, a clinic, a collective. Choose a name that appeals to you. Meet once a week and read and discuss one another's writing. You'll find that other student writers will be both your most critical and your most sympathetic readers. That's because they're trying to be writers, too. They know what you're going through.

From time to time, you and the other members of your writing group may want to present your work to a larger audience. That way you can find out how people other than writers react to what you're writing.

poetry reading

Skill in reading your poems and stories aloud may be one of your best routes to a general audience. Poets, particularly, are often called on to give public readings of their work. These readings are popular because hearing writers read their own poems makes these poems more convincing. You know you're hearing words and phrases emphasized the way the writer wants them to be. It's almost as if you are hearing the poem being born.

> **The experience of . . . the poetry reading is dynamic to many people who would not have had that experience reading the poems on the page.**
> **—Diane Wakoski**

You might want to get together with some other students to test your skill in the oral interpretation of your own work. Plan a poetry reading in your school auditorium. Select your best poems. You can include one or two very short stories or sketches as well.

Arrange the selections to make an interesting program. You can put similar poems together. Or you can make use of the principle of contrast. You can start, for instance, with a group of light or funny poems, move on to ones that express heavier emotions—angry poems, sad poems—and then finish off with a group of happy poems.

If you like, you can use music to help create the mood for each group of poems. Get some students to play live music. Otherwise, use records. At the end of the reading, you can invite the audience to ask you questions about your work. This can be valuable to you. You can learn what kind of impact your writing has had on the audience. You may even get some new insights into what your poems mean. And you may collect some suggestions for rewriting your poems.

the writing lab

If your school has a writing lab, you may have the chance to participate. The writing lab in many schools is a room set aside from the regular classrooms and equipped not only with tables and chairs and display areas but also with personal computers, software, and printers. Using a word-processing program for prewriting, composing, and especially revising is not only a great time-saver but fun, too. Imagine the great printouts you can get of concrete poems.

Laurence Risser

In some writing labs computer programs help you hone specific writing skills. In others the thrust is on creative and experimental writing. You may work, for instance, with a small group composing a collective poem, each student contributing a line or two. You may be involved in a journalism assignment, doing research and interviews in your community, possibly even working with your local newspaper.

The possibilities of the writing lab are almost endless. But one advantage overrides all the others: you get to work intensively on a project, use the feedback of your classmates and instructor to revise and polish, and then publish what you have written.

the literary magazine

Your school may have a magazine that publishes creative writing. If so, you can submit your poems or stories or plays to that publication. Follow the same procedures for preparing your manuscript that you would use if you were sending it to a professional publication.

If you don't have a literary magazine in your school, you may want to start one. You and the other students in your creative writing class could begin publication in a modest way. Form an editorial board to choose the best material from what you've written. Arrange the stories and poems and plays in an effective order. Then type them on ditto masters or mimeograph stencils. Run off as many copies as you think you'll have readers. It's better to have too few than too many. Distribute them at a time when students will be likely to read them—in the cafeteria during lunch, during homeroom.

If your trial magazine catches on, you can make more of a production of it. You can hold a contest to choose a name for the magazine. This will stimulate student interest. You can also circulate a questionnaire to students. That way you can find out what your readers want in a magazine and how much they might be willing to pay. It's a good means of recruiting staff members for the magazine, too. On the following pages you'll find a sample questionnaire. You can use it or devise one of your own.

Try to get student writing from the whole school, maybe even hold a writing contest with prizes to be awarded during a school assembly. You can also include student artwork and photographs to make the magazine visually interesting.

Eventually, you'll need to decide whether or not you want to have your magazine professionally printed. Professional printing is more expensive. And it will probably mean that you have to sell advertising to pay the printer's bill. But it will give you the experience of using professional production techniques for choosing typefaces, paper, and colors; designing layouts; handling photographs; marking copy for the typesetter; reading proofs; and creating and selling ads.

To All Students:

Within the next few weeks, a student literary magazine will make its appearance. We need your suggestions to help make the magazine a success.

1. First of all, we'd like you to help us choose a name for the magazine. Write your choice here: _____. If you have several suggestions, list them on the back.

2. We want to be sure that you enjoy reading the magazine. So we'd like you to help us decide what should go into it. (Please rank in the order of preference.)

	Not interested			Very interested		
Poetry	1	2	3	4	5	6
Short Stories	1	2	3	4	5	6
Plays	1	2	3	4	5	6
Informal Essays	1	2	3	4	5	6
Feature Stories	1	2	3	4	5	6
Book Reviews	1	2	3	4	5	6
Movie Reviews	1	2	3	4	5	6
Music, Dance, and Art Reviews	1	2	3	4	5	6
Humor	1	2	3	4	5	6
Cartoons	1	2	3	4	5	6
Photo Essays	1	2	3	4	5	6
Student Art (other than illustrations of stories and poems)	1	2	3	4	5	6
Illustrative Art	1	2	3	4	5	6
Classified Advertising	1	2	3	4	5	6
Other _____	1	2	3	4	5	6

3. Check what you consider a reasonable price for a 50-page magazine: _____ $1.50 _____ $2.50 _____ $3.50

4. In order to decide how many copies of the magazine to produce, we need a rough idea of the magazine's probably circulation. Do you think that you would buy a copy?

_____Yes _____No _____Maybe

5. We need advice, but we also need active help. If you would like to be a member of the magazine staff, check the job you think you could do most effectively:

_____Editor _____Illustrator

_____Managing Editor _____Photographer

_____Copy Editor _____Paste-up Artist

_____Art Director _____Manuscript Typist

_____Production Supervisor _____Proofreader

_____Advertising Director _____Business Manager

_____Advertising Production Manager _____Promotion Director

_____Advertising Space Salesperson _____Circulation Director

6. Perhaps you have a manuscript or a drawing or a photo you would like to submit to the magazine right away. If so, fill out the following, attach your contribution to this questionnaire, and send both to:

Literary Magazine, Room _____, Attention: _____

Title _____

Type (for example, a short story) _____

Number of words _____

Name _____

Year in school _____ Homeroom _____

Your work will be considered for publication only if you sign

this pledge:

I hereby certify that this is my original idea and work.

_____
Student's Signature

Manuscripts, artwork, and photographs must be submitted

by _____.
        Date

writers are readers

If you think you want to stick with writing for a while, there are two things you must keep on doing: Write a lot. Read a lot. The best way to connect with the craft of good writing is to read good writers. They're your best teachers. They can't give you the experiences to write about. Nor can they pass on the creative spark. But they can show you how they did it. And a great deal can be absorbed unconsciously. So read the great storytellers, poets, playwrights, journalists of the past and the present. Read writers who are publishing now in magazines like *Esquire, The Atlantic, Harper's, The New Yorker*. Read the O. Henry Prize collections that come out each year and Martha Foley's annual collection, *The Best American Short Stories*. See if your library or bookstore carries any literary magazines, quarterlies, or underground periodicals that include fiction and poetry. The wider your reading tastes, the more you will become aware of the many possibilities in imaginative writing. You may want to dig a little deeper into the technical aspects of a particular form—poetry, short story, play, or the New Journalism. Maybe you want to read what writers have to say about their own writing. Here are some books and films that will give you more insight into the craft of creative writing.

poetry

Allen, Walter, ed. *The Writer on His Art.* New York: McGraw, Hill, 1948. *Comments by many poets collected under several headings, including Inspiration and Calculation, The Poet's Subject, The Poet's Style, Rhythm, Rhyme and Diction, and Poetry and Symbolism.*

Armour, Richard. *Writing Light Verse and Prose Humor.* Boston: The Writer, Inc., 1958. *Practical advice on writing humor.*

Barry, Elaine. *Robert Frost on Writing.* Rutgers, N.Y.: Rutgers, 1974. *A collection of letters, prefaces, interviews, and lectures in which Frost discusses poets and the craft of poetry.*

Bogan, Louise. *What the Woman Lived: Selected Letters of Louise Bogan, 1920–1970.* Ruth Limmer, ed. New York: Harcourt, Brace, Jovanovich, 1973. *Includes informal comments by Bogan on her own writing and on the work of other poets.*

Concrete Poetry. Pyramid Films. Santa Monica, Calif. *Poems from Emmett Williams'* An Anthology of Concrete Poetry *are visualized. 12 minutes.*

Haiku. ACI Films, Inc. New York. *Blend of images and music giving history and examples of haiku poetry. 18 minutes. Color.*

Hughes, Ted. *Poetry Is.* Garden City, N.Y.: Doubleday, 1967. *Informal introduction to poetry writing by a poet. Sections include Capturing Animals, Wind and Weather, Writing About People, Learning to Think, Writing About Landscape, Meet My Folks, Moon Creatures.*

Rilke, Rainier Maria. *Letters to a Young Poet.* tr. M.D. Herter Norton. New York: Norton, 1969. *A book to inspire the young poet rather than to give technical advice.*

drama

Battcock, Gregory, and Nickas, Robert, eds. *The Art of Performance, A Critical Anthology.* New York, E.P. Dutton, Inc., 1984. *A collection of essays on performance art by critics and artists.*

Cole, Toby, ed. *Playwrights on Playwriting.* New York: Hill and Wang, 1961. *Philosophical and technical discussions about writing for the theater by practicing dramatists.*

Kerr, Walter. *How Not to Write a Play.* Boston: The Writer, Inc., 1955. *Some common pitfalls in playwriting.*

Lorraine Hansberry: The Black Experience in the Creation of Drama. Films for the Humanities, Inc. Princeton, N.J. *Hansberry talks about her work as a playwright.*

Olson, Elder. *Tragedy and the Theory of Drama.* Detroit: Wayne State University Press, 1961. *Insight into the techniques of shaping incidents, creating character, and indicating offstage action.*

Rosenheim, Edward W., Jr. *What Happens in Literature.* Chicago: The University of Chicago Press, 1960. *Detailed discussion in third chapter of what makes writing for the theater different from writing other fiction.*

The Short Play Showcase of Films. Encyclopaedia Britannica Educational Corporation, Chicago. *Thornton Wilder's Theater of Imagination represented by* The Long Christmas Dinner. *The Theater of the Absurd represented by Ionesco's* The New Tenant. *Naturalism represented by Synge's* The Well of the Saints.

short story

Bowen, Elizabeth. *Collected Impressions.* London: Longmans, 1950. *"Notes on Writing a Novel" contains technical advice also useful to short-story writers.*

Cather, Willa. *On Writing.* New York: Knopf, 1949. *Essays on individual writers—Sarah Orne Jewett, Stephen Crane, and Katherine Mansfield—contain practical advice for short-story writers.*

Chekhov, Anton. *Letters on the Short Story, the Drama and Other Literary Topics.* Louis S. Friedland, ed. New York: Blom, 1965.

Many of these letters were written to young short-story writers and playwrights who asked Chekhov for advice.

The LCA Short Story Library Series. Coronet/MTI Film and Video, Deer-field, Illinois. *A collection of outstanding film productions of classic short stories, reflecting a wide range of themes, narrative voices, and literary styles.*

Lubbock, Percy. *The Craft of Fiction.* New York: Viking, 1921. *Detailed study of point of view in fiction.*

Mansfield, Katherine. *Journal of Katherine Mansfield.* John M. Murry, ed. New York: Fertig, 1975. Reprint of 1927 edition. *Notes for stories, fragments of diaries, unmailed letters, impressions by a short-story writer.*

Maugham, W. Somerset. *Writer's Notebook.* London: Heinemann, 1949. *What Maugham calls his "storehouse of materials for future use." Impressions of persons and places, feelings, thoughts.*

Mirrielees, Edith Ronald. *Story Writing.* New York: Viking, 1962. *Practical advice from John Steinbeck's creative writing teacher. Includes chapters on repetition, time, points of observation, implication, characterization, dialogue, and revision.*

Moffett, James, and Kenneth R. McElheny. *Points of View: An Anthology of Short Stories.* New York: Mentor, 1966. *Stories selected to show variety in point of view. Good introductory material in each section.*

Story of a Writer. Sterling Educational Films. New York. *A documentary on the work of Ray Bradbury.*

Tchudi, Susan & Stephen. *The Young Writer's Handbook.* New York: Charles Scribner's Sons, 1984. *A guide to developing a writing style and keeping a writer's journal.*

Vivante, Arturo. *Writing Fiction.* Boston: The Writer, Inc. Publishers, 1980. *Professional advice on effective characterization, use of dialogue, different points of view, and development of theme.*

Wharton, Edith. *The Writing of Fiction.* New York: Octagon, 1967. *In chapter on short-story writing, Wharton discusses choice of subject, point of view, short-story beginnings and endings, importance of economy in short stories.*

Woolf, Virginia. *A Writer's Diary: Being Extracts from the Diary of Virginia Woolf.* Leonard Woolf, ed. New York: Harcourt, Brace, Jovanovich, 1973. *Woolf's comments on her own work in progress and on other writers.*

Writers at Work: The Paris Review Interviews. Malcolm Cowley, ed. New York: Viking.

Series 1, 1958, includes interviews with E. M. Forster, François Mauriac, Joyce Cary, Dorothy Parker, James Thurber, Thornton Wilder, William Faulkner, Georges Simenon, Frank O'Connor, Robert Penn Warren, Alberto Moravio, Nelson Algren, Angus Wilson, William Styron, Truman Capote, and Françoise Sagan. Series 2, 1965, includes interviews with Robert Frost, Ezra Pound, Marianne Moore, T. S. Eliot, Boris Pasternak, Katherine Anne Porter, Henry Miller, Aldous Huxley, Ernest Hemingway, S. J. Perelman, Lawrence Durrell, Mary McCarthy, Ralph Ellison, and Robert Lowell. Series 3, 1968, includes William Carlos Williams, Jean Cocteau, Louis Ferdinand Celine, Evelyn Waugh, Lillian Hellman, William Burroughs, Saul Bellow, Arthur Miller, James Jones, Norman Mailer, Allen Ginsberg, Edward Albee, and Harold Pinter.

Writing Series. Coronet/MTI Film and Video. Deerfield, Illinois. *Video series including* Getting Ideas to Write About *and* Holding Them Spellbound, *films on writing short stories.*

new journalism

Didion, Joan. *Slouching Towards Bethlehem.* New York: Farrar, Straus, & Giroux, 1968. *A collection of New Journalism pieces by Joan Didion, all with California settings.*

Hayes, Harold. *Smiling Through the Apocalypse.* New York: Dell, 1971. *A collection of New Journalism pieces published in* Esquire *during the 1960s.*

Hills, Rust. *writing in general and the short story in particular: An Informal Textbook.* New York: Bantam Books, 1977. *A writing guide that includes information on the "New Journalism," the "New Fiction," and the "New Criticism."*

Ross, Lillian. *Talk Stories.* New York: Simon and Schuster, 1966. *A collection of Ross's Talk of the Town columns from* The New Yorker. *Includes individual profiles and group portraits.*

Talese, Gay. *Fame and Obscurity: Portraits.* Cleveland: World, 1970. *New Journalism profiles of both celebrities and obscure people.*

Wolfe, Tom. *The New Journalism.* With an anthology edited by Tom Wolfe and E. W. Johnson. New York: Harper and Row, 1973. *Tom Wolfe's own analysis of the New Journalism scene.*

Some Technical Aspects of Verse

Knowing the technical terms for the different kinds of rhyme or for the different stanza forms is not the same as knowing how to put a poem together. But these terms are useful. And knowing them is a help not only in talking about verse but in understanding how it works.

Rhyme

Both masculine and feminine rhymes are considered full rhymes. The only difference between them, as you learned in Chapter 3, is that the final syllables in feminine rhymes are unstressed. So, *go/show* are masculine rhymes. And *sorrow/borrow* are feminine rhymes.

Full rhyme is the usual rhyme in English poetry. But it is not the only kind. In addition to full rhyme, there is sight rhyme, assonance, consonance, and identical rhyme. Mostly, these other kinds of rhyme are used to achieve variety and avoid the heavy effect that continuous full rhyme sometimes produces.

Sight rhyme, or eye rhyme, involves using words that look as though they rhyme. But when you pronounce them, they really don't rhyme. Here is Robert Graves using sight rhyme. The words in italics are sight rhymes.

> Trampled by no hard hooves, stained with no *blood*,
> Bold, immortal country whose hill tops have *stood*.

Other sight rhymes, like *blood/stood*, are *own/crown*, *through/plough*, and *love/prove*. However, in reading earlier poets, you can't always be sure that a sight rhyme was intended. For instance, in Alexander Pope's time, the word *tea* was pronounced to rhyme with *may*. So in the following lines, *obey/tea* were full rhymes. Changes in pronunciation have produced a sight rhyme.

> Here thou, great Anna! whom three realms *obey*,
> Dost sometimes counsel take—and sometimes *tea*.

Assonance is partial rhyme—the consonant sounds that follow the vowels are different. With full rhyme both the vowel sounds and the consonant sounds that follow them are the same. The words *cat* and *rat* are examples of full rhyme. The words *cat* and *man* are examples of assonance. Here's another example of assonance, taken from Coleridge's *Rime of the Ancient Mariner:*

> This seraph-band, each waved his *hand,*
> No voice did they impart—
> No voice; but O, the silence *sank*
> Like music on my heart.

Consonance, also called slant rhyme, couples words in which the vowel sounds differ, but the consonant sounds that follow them are the same. Examples of consonance are *add/read* and *teeth/death.* In this couplet, William Blake uses consonance:

> A horse misused upon the *road*
> Calls to heaven for human *blood.*

At one time, identical rhyme was thought to be a mistake. Critics, but not practicing poets, said that it wasn't a true rhyme, meaning a full rhyme. But so many accomplished poets, both modern and traditional, have used this kind of rhyme, and used it well, that it seems a little foolish to call identical rhyme a mistake. Here, for example, is Tennyson using it:

> For some were hung with arras green and *blue.*
> Showing a gaudy summer morn,
> Where with puffed cheek the belted hunter *blew*
> His wreathed bugle horn.

The words *blue/blew* are spelled differently, but pronounced the same. This is identical rhyme. Other identical rhymes are *rain/reign, right/write,* and *see/sea.*

Most rhymes in English are masculine. That is, the final, stressed syllable of one word rhymes with the final, stressed syllable of another. Feminine rhymes, in which the final two syllables of each word rhyme, occur less often. Triple, or three-syllable, rhymes are even rarer. Mainly, they are used for humorous effect, as in the following lines by Ogden Nash:

One thing that literature would be greatly
   the *better for*
Would be more restricted employment by authors of
   simile and *metaphor.*

Most rhymes occur at the ends of lines. But some poets also use internal rhyme. That is, they rhyme words within a line, as Coleridge did here:

This hermit *good* lives in that *wood*

Some English words are difficult to rhyme. For instance, the only full rhyme for *strength* is *length.* The word *courage* rhymes only with *demurrage,* a fee paid for failing to unload freight within an agreed upon time.

And here are some English words that have no full rhymes:

warmth	gulf	pint	breadth	bilge
wolf	width	mouth	wasp	scarce

Stanza Forms

Just as prose has paragraphs, poetry has stanzas. These are units of two or more lines of verse. The names for these units refer to the number of lines they contain:

couplet: two lines	sestet: six lines
tercet: three lines	septet: seven lines
quatrain: four lines	octave: eight lines
quintet: five lines	

In addition to these general names, certain stanza forms also have specific names. These refer not only to the number of lines but often to the rhyme scheme and the meter as well. For instance, the term *heroic couplet* refers to two rhymed lines of verse written in iambic pentameter. Here's an example of a heroic couplet:

Behold the child, by nature's kindly law,
Pleased with a rattle, tickled with a straw.
   —Alexander Pope

This kind of couplet is also called a closed couplet. It is "closed" in the sense that its meaning is completed in the two lines. In contrast, here are two couplets from another poem. Notice that the meaning is not completed in the first couplet, but runs on into the second:

> You faded. I never knew
> How to unfold as flowers do,
>
> Or how to nourish anything
> To make it grow. I wound a wing
> —*Genevieve Taggard*

These are called open couplets.

Whether open or closed, both kinds of couplets consist of two rhymed lines of verse in matching meter. This is what makes them couplets and marks them off as independent units. A pair of couplets, for instance, do not add up to a quatrain. They remain a pair of couplets.

Probably the most frequently used stanza form in English is the quatrain, which shows many variations in rhyme and meter. In one kind of quatrain, the ballad stanza, the second and fourth lines are rhymed, while the first and third are left unrhymed:

> None of my gold now you shall have,   **a**
> Nor likewise of my fee;   **b**
> For I am come to see you hanged,   **c**
> And hanged you shall be.   **b**

Notice that the rhyme scheme for this stanza has been marked by letters of the alphabet. The first rhyme word is marked *a*, the second *b*, and the third *c*. If the stanza were longer and had more rhymes, you would simply continue through the alphabet until all the rhymes had been accounted for.

You may also have noticed that the second and fourth lines of this stanza have been indented, or moved over, from the left-hand margin. This is done to guide the reader's eye to the lines that rhyme. Generally, indention in poetry works this way: *a*-rhymed lines begin at the left-hand margin; *b*-rhymed lines are indented; *c*-rhymed lines come back to the left-hand margin. The *c*-rhymed lines come back to the left to keep the poem from drifting across the page. Also, this prevents having to break long lines in two to make them fit on the page.

Here is another quatrain in which the rhymes are *a-b-a-b*. Though this stanza form has no specific name, it is used even more often than the ballad stanza.

> Ah, did you once see Shelley plain,
> And did he stop and speak to you,
> And did you speak to him again?
> How strange it seems and new!
> —*Robert Browning*

Notice that each new line, whether in a quatrain or a couplet, begins with a capital letter. This is standard practice in traditional poems. However, when a line is too long to fit on the page, part of the line must be carried over. Since this carried-over part is not really a new line, but a continuation of the previous line, it begins with a small letter and is indented. Here, as an illustration, is a quintet, or five-line stanza. Notice that the long fifth line has been carried over.

> Before ever land was,
> Before ever the sea,
> Or soft hair of the grass,
> Or fair limbs of the tree,
> Or the flesh-colored fruit of my branches, I was, and thy
> soul was in me.
> —*A. C. Swinburne*

The examples of stanza forms shown thus far have all been taken from longer poems. But a stanza may be a complete poem in itself. Here, for example, is a quintet that is a complete poem. It's called a limerick:

> There once was a man from Nantucket
> Who kept all his cash in a bucket;
> But his daughter named Nan
> Ran away with a man,
> And as for the bucket, Nantucket.

And here is another five-line stanza that is a complete poem. It's called a cinquain:

Just now,
Out of the strange
Still dusk—as strange, as still—
A white moth flew. Why am I grown
So cold?

—Adelaide Crapsey

The sestet, or six-line stanza, also comes in a variety of meters and rhyme schemes. Here are two examples with their rhymes indicated. The first is taken from a poem by Wordsworth:

I wandered lonely as a cloud	a
That floats on high o'er vales and hills,	b
When all at once I saw a crowd,	a
A host of golden daffodils;	b
Beside the lake, beneath the trees,	c
Fluttering and dancing in the breeze.	c

The second is from a poem by Robert Burns and is written in a Scottish dialect:

Still thou are blest compared wi' me!	a
The present only toucheth thee:	a
But oh! I backward cast my e'e	a
On prospects drear!	b
An' forward tho' I canna see,	a
I guess an' fear!	b

The term *sestet* is also used to refer to the last six lines of a sonnet.

The septet is not a much-used stanza form. Its most well known variety is rhyme royal, named for James I of Scotland, who was both a poet and a king. Rhyme royal has also been used by Chaucer, by Shakespeare, and, in more recent times, by John Masefield. It is a seven-line stanza written in iambic pentameter and rhyming *a-b-a-b-b-c-c*. Here is an example:

Of Heaven or Hell I have no power to sing,
I cannot ease the burden of your fears,
Or make quick-coming death a little thing,
Or bring again the pleasure of past years,
Nor for my words shall ye forget your tears,

Or hope again, for aught that I can say,
The idle singer of an empty day.

—*William Morris*

The octave, an eight-line stanza, was a favorite of the Romantic poets, particularly Keats, Byron, and Shelley. The following octave is taken from a poem by Shelley:

When the lamp is shattered,	**a**
The light in the dust lies dead—	**b**
When the cloud is scattered,	**a**
The rainbow's glory is shed.	**b**
When the lute is broken,	**c**
Sweet tones are remembered not;	**d**
When the lips have spoken,	**c**
Loved accents are soon forgot.	**d**

Among the modern poets, E. A. Robinson, Robert Frost, and W. B. Yeats have used the octave. Generally speaking, these poets have written octaves in iambic pentameter, though their rhyme schemes have varied considerably.

The term *octave* also refers to the first eight lines of a sonnet. A sonnet is a fourteen-line poem usually written in iambic pentameter and following one of two basic forms—the Italian or the English.

The Italian form of the sonnet is divided into two parts. The first part is the octave and consists of eight lines that rhyme *a-b-b-a-a-b-b-a*. The second part is the sestet and consists of six lines that rhyme either *c-d-e-c-d-e* or *c-d-c-d-c-d*. There is a break in thought between the octave and the sestet. When an Italian sonnet is printed, extra space is usually put between the two parts to mark this break. An example of the Italian sonnet follows:

Down to the Puritan marrow of my bones	**a**
There's something in this richness that I hate.	**b**
I love the look, austere, immaculate,	**b**
Of landscapes drawn in pearly monotones.	**a**
There's something in my very blood that owns	**a**
Bare hills, cold silver on a sky of slate,	**b**
A thread of water, churned to milky spate	**b**
Streaming through slanted pastures fenced with stones.	**a**

240

I love those skies, thin blue or snowy gray,	c
Those fields sparse-planted, rendering meagre sheaves;	d
That spring, briefer than apple-blossom's breath,	e
Summer, so much too beautiful to stay,	c
Swift autumn, like a bonfire of leaves,	d
And sleepy winter, like the sleep of death.	e

—Elinor Wylie

This form is also called the Petrarchan sonnet after the fourteenth-century Francesco Petrarch, its most famous practitioner.

The English sonnet, which is also called the Shakespearean sonnet, consists of three quatrains, each with its own rhyme scheme, plus a couplet. The couplet acts as a sort of punch line, a concise summing-up of what has gone before.

Shall I compare thee to a summer's day?	a
Thou are more lovely and more temperate:	b
Rough winds do shake the darling buds of May,	a
And summer's lease hath all too short a date:	b
Sometime too hot the eye of heaven shines,	c
And often is his gold complexion dimmed:	d
And every fair from fair sometime declines,	c
By chance, or nature's changing course, untrimmed.	d
But thy eternal summer shall not fade	e
Nor lose possession of that fair thou owest;	f
Nor shall Death brag thou wanderest in his shade,	e
When in eternal lines to time thou growest:	f
So long as men can breathe, or eyes can see,	g
So long lives this, and this gives life to thee.	g

—William Shakespeare

A common variation of each of these basic forms exists. The Miltonic sonnet is a variation of the Italian sonnet. Instead of dividing his sonnets into two parts, as Petrarch had done, John Milton ran his thought without a break through the entire fourteen lines. Thus, the contrast between the octave and the sestet disappears in the Miltonic sonnet.

The Spenserian sonnet is a variation of the English sonnet. Though he divided his sonnets into three quatrains and a couplet, Edmund Spenser linked his quatrains closer together by using two fewer rhymes than Shakespeare.

Study the following chart. It summarizes the basic sonnet forms and their important variations.

BASIC SONNET FORMS

	Italian (Petrarchan)	Miltonic		English (Shakespearean)	Spenserian
octave	a	a		quatrain a	a
	b	b		b	b
	b	b		a	a
	a	a		b	b
	a	a			
	b	b		quatrain c	b
	b	b		d	c
	a	a		c	b
	(break)	(no break)		d	c
sestet	c	c	c	quatrain e	c
	d	d	d	f	d
	e	c or c		e	c
	c	d	d	f	d
	d	c	e		
	e	d	e	couplet g	e
				g	e
number of rhymes	5	4	5	7	5

The stanza forms that have been described are all traditional. But stanzas also occur in free verse. In free verse the stanza divisions are often irregular and almost always based on personal judgment. The same holds true for indention, capitalization, and punctuation in free verse. You might think, then, that a poet is forced to choose between traditional forms and free verse and that most modern poets would choose free verse. Actually, some of the most accomplished modern poets use both. E. E. Cummings and W. H. Auden, to name only two, have written sonnets as well as free-verse forms. A poet is free to choose whatever form best expresses his or her ideas.

Some Technical Aspects of Dialogue

Dialogue is talk between two or more people. Obviously, creating dialogue that is lifelike and crisp is a dramatist's major task. Not so obviously, it is also part of the job of the short-story writer and even, sometimes, of the journalist.

Diction

The words you put into the mouths of your characters should reflect the kinds of persons you imagine them to be. Their words should reflect their education, social status, job.

Ordinarily, you would not make an auto mechanic sound like a university president, unless, say, you were after a humorous effect. A soldier, for instance, should sound like a soldier: "The new C.O.? Why, he's about as useful as rust in the barrel of an M 16."

But there's more to writing dialogue than being realistic. There's an art to it. Your dialogue must not only be true to your characters' ways of speaking, it must also be clear to your audience. Each line of dialogue must make sense, at least in a general way, without reference to any special knowledge.

Then what about using terms like *C.O.* and *M 16?* Isn't it likely that a part of your audience will not know that the first term means "commanding officer" and that the second is a kind of rifle? Probably. So, to overcome this problem, you must provide clues. The word *useful, rust,* and *barrel* are clues that point to the general meaning of this line. Anyone in the audience will know that the soldier is not paying a compliment.

Pace

A long speech in a story or a play is not one that runs on for pages. Don't even think about letting one of your characters talk that much. A long speech is anything over five or six sentences.

In general, long speeches tend to slow the pace of your dialogue. If you find that you are putting long speeches into the mouths of your characters, take a second look at what you have written. See if there aren't ways of breaking up these speeches. You might, for instance, have a character interrupt a long speech with a question.

The pace of your characters' dialogue should mirror their personalities. A stubborn person will probably speak in clipped, determined phrases: "Can't be done," "Not interested." A shy person, on the other hand, may wander and hesitate, may use a lot of "ah's" and "uh's." A happy person will speak rapidly, maybe mix up the order of words, and run them together. A sad person will speak slowly and deliberately, drawing the words out.

Coherence

Dialogue should be true to life. But it cannot be exactly true. Real speech is often aimless, halting, unfinished. Real speech in a story or a play would be boring and hard to follow. The trick is to write dialogue that seems real, but that is easy for the audience to follow.

One device that helps knit lines of dialogue together is repetition. One character picks up on what another has just said. As an illustration, here's a single-word repetition from a play by Susan Glaspell:

> HENRIETTA: You're no longer open to new ideas. You won't listen to a word about psychoanalysis.
> STEVE: A word! I've listened to volumes.

And here, from a play by G. B. Shaw, is a repetition using a group of words:

> SWINDON: (Severely) Do you mean to deny that you are a rebel?
> RICHARD: I am an American, sir.
> SWINDON: What do you expect me to think of that speech, Mr. Anderson?
> RICHARD: I never expect a soldier to think, sir.

Still another way to tie lines of dialogue together is with interruptions. One character breaks in on another, completing the first character's line:

> SENATOR DURKIN: If only we could get enough—
> BOSS RILEY: Hard cash?

244

SENATOR DURKIN:—party support.

Boss RILEY: The two are the same, Senator.

If you use these devices and your dialogue sounds wrong, somehow disjointed, then maybe your ideas don't go together. And maybe you should start over and rewrite your dialogue, instead of trying to patch it.

Tags

In writing dialogue for a short story, you start a new paragraph each time the speaker changes. Be careful not to clutter the dialogue with long tags. Usually, "he said" or "she said" is enough. Some beginning writers throw their dialogue off-balance with elaborate tags like these:

"You've got it," spat Phil with venom.

"That's stupid," hissed Julia viciously.

These colorful verbs and qualifiers cloud what the characters actually said. They get in the way. Often, if you've really matched your characters and their ways of speaking, you won't need any tags at all. Look at the dialogue in the short stories of John O'Hara if you want to see how this is done.

Some Technical Aspects of Staging

Closet drama is a special kind of drama. What's special about it is that it's not written to be performed on a stage. It's simply fiction, or more often, poetry, written in the form of a drama, because the writer felt that that was the most effective way to tell a particular story. John Milton's tragedy, *Samson Agonistes*, is a famous example.

Most drama, however, is written to be performed, just as music is written to be played. So, if you are going to write a play, you should be aware of the different kinds of stages available. Also, you should have some idea of the possibilities and the restrictions of each kind of stage. And you should know the names of the various positions on those stages. That way, you can visualize a particular kind of stage as you write your play. This will help you write clear directions for the placement of scenery and the movement of your characters.

Proscenium Stage

The most common kind of stage is called the proscenium, or picture-frame, stage. The opening through which the audience looks at the play forms a frame like the frame around a painting. In many older theaters, this frame—actually, an arch—is even decorated like a picture frame. The Auditorium Theater in Chicago,

designed by famed architect Louis Sullivan, has one of the most elaborately decorated proscenium arches. A proscenium stage also has a curtain that can be opened and closed. It may be closed to allow for a change of scenery, to show passage of time, or simply to indicate the act or scene divisions of the play.

One restriction of the proscenium stage is that the actors can't really face one another. If two characters are supposed to be having an argument, the actors can only create the illusion of facing each other. They must turn partly toward the audience. Otherwise, the audience won't be able to see their faces and may not hear what they're saying. If the theater is small and the audience close to the stage, the actors have greater flexibility. They can even at times turn their backs toward the audience. But in a large theater, especially one with an orchestra pit between the stage and the audience, the actors need to address the audience as directly as they can.

Directions for actors' movements on the stage are known as blocking. On the proscenium stage, blocking is indicated in terms of nine basic positions:

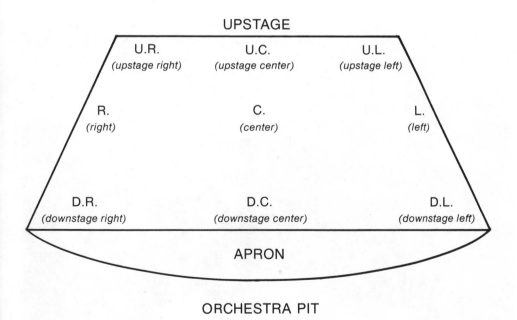

Notice that the directions *left* and *right* mean left and right from the viewpoint of the actors, not of the audience. The actors enter or leave the stage by way of the wings (sides) or at the back, depending on the location of the doors or other openings in the set.

No positions are given for the curved area of the stage, called the apron, that protrudes beyond the proscenium arch. That's because the traditional rules of the proscenium stage call for the actors to stay within the picture frame.

Arena Stage

Unlike the proscenium stage, the arena stage is not a raised platform. It's just an open space at floor level in the center of an auditorium. The audience sits in seats arranged like bleachers around the four sides of the acting area. The seating in most arena theaters is limited to about 200. But this brings the audience close enough to the actors to see subtle changes of expression and gestures.

Production of Shakespeare's *The Taming of the Shrew*.
George de Vincent, courtesy Arena Stage, Washington D

Because the audience surrounds the stage, only a limited amount of scenery can be used. And what there is must be arranged so that it doesn't interfere with anyone's view of the acting area. Usually, the way to do this is to keep the scenery and stage furniture low. But high, see-through structures can also work well. Look at the photograph of the Arena Stage, Washington, D.C., and you'll see how a symbolic setting was created for Shakespeare's *The Taming of the Shrew* with simple scaffolding.

The blocking must be planned so that the important scenes aren't played to only one or two sides of the house. Actually, this is not as difficult as it may seem. To begin with, the actors won't all be facing the same way, as they usually are on a proscenium stage. Each one may be facing a different direction. So, at a given moment, a member of the audience may see one actor from the front, two others in profile, and a fourth from the back. The actors alternate their positions within a scene and from scene to scene in order that one section of the audience doesn't see the same character's back throughout the play.

If you want to include stage directions keyed to arena staging in your playscript, you can't refer to the positions on a proscenium stage. That's because there is no left or right on an arena stage, no upstage or downstage. On an arena stage the positions are labeled in terms of the center of the stage (C) and the four corners (W, X, Y, and Z):

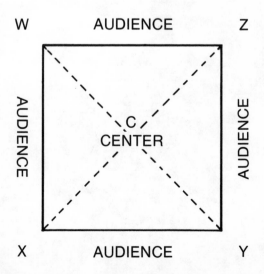

249

The positions on the lines that run from the center to each of the four corners are the ones where the actors can be seen by the largest number of people.

Because there is no curtain, scene changes must be made either in darkness or in view of the audience. Pieces of scenery and furniture are moved through the aisles of the theater. The aisles are also used by the actors to enter or to leave the stage. The speed of the entrances and exits can be controlled by lighting. If you want an actress to make a quick exit, you can indicate that the house should be plunged into darkness the minute she's off the acting area. Should the occasion arise, you can even use the aisles as streets. You can create the effect of crowds of people rushing angrily to the center of town, for example, by having actors converge on the acting area from all four corners.

Platform Stage

The platform stage combines features of both the proscenium stage and the arena stage. Imagine that the apron of the proscenium stage has been extended so that it juts out into the audience.

Photo courtesy of The Guthrie Theater

The audience now sits on three sides of the acting area, in steeply rising banks of seats, and can watch the actors at close range. A theater with a platform stage can be quite large and still preserve the intimacy of arena staging. The Guthrie Theater in Minneapolis, for example, seats nearly 1,500 people. Yet no seat is more than fifty-two feet from the center of the stage.

The platform stage is similar to the stage used in Shakespeare's Globe Theatre. It provides a structure to move about on rather than a background to play in front of. At the back there may be several platforms at different levels, connected by stairs or ramps. On this kind of stage, it's possible to move rapidly from scene to scene. A scene can finish on one platform, and the next one can immediately begin on another level. The platform stage also offers the greatest flexibility for entrances and exits. The Shakespeare Festival Theatre in Stratford, Ontario, for example, has sixteen different entrances to the stage, counting the trapdoor in the stage floor.

The platform stage is thus well suited to plays with many scene changes, large casts, and lots of movement.

Index

Shelley, Percy Bysshe, 77, 240
Short story writing
  climax in, 159
  compactness in, 161
  completeness in, 157–159, 165–166
  creating suspense, 157–159,
    165–166
  point of view in, 169–176, 182
  proportion in, 160–161, 165–166
  surprise ending in, 166–169
Simile, 70–72
Sonnet, 74, 239, 240–242
Sound words, 40–41
Sources of ideas
  clothing, 49–50
  doodle chart, 41
  drawings, 35
  food, 50–53
  likes and dislikes, 42–43
  newspapers and magazines, 32
  photographs, 45–48, 51
  pictures, 34
  proverbs, 43–44
  quotations, 43–44
Stage directions, 134–135, 246–251
Stage positions. *See* Blocking.
Stages, types of
  arena, 248–250
  platform, 250–251
  proscenium, 246–248
Stanza forms
  ballad stanza, 237
  clerihew, 36
  couplet, 236–237
  haiku, 81
  rhyme royal, 239–240
  sonnet, 74, 239, 240–242
Steinberg, Saul, 49
Stryk, Lucien, 67
Subjects for writing. *See* Sources
    for ideas.
Suspense
  in playwriting, 127–130
  in short story writing, 157–159,
    165–166

Sutheim, Susan, 88
Swinburne, A. C., 238
Symbols, 118–119

Taggard, Genevieve, 237
Tennyson, Alfred, 235

Vonnegut, Kurt, Jr., 19

Warm-ups
  dialogue between unlikes, 31–32
  doodle chart, 41
  familiar opening lines, 38
  fantasies with words, 49
  happenings, 37–38
  likes and dislikes, 42–43
  name poetry, 36
  proverbs and quotations, 43–44
  public versus private, 44
  reacting to a newspaper article, 32
  sound words, 40–41
  story fill-in, 28–29
  time capsule, 27–28
  weird invitations, 39–40
  writing about clothes, 49
  writing about food, 50–53
  writing about pictures, 34–36
  writing from photos, 45–48
Welty, Eudora, 108, 109
Williams, William Carlos, 67
Wolfe, Humbert, 70
Wolfe, Tom, 190, 196–198
Word museum, 224–225
Wordsworth, William, 239
Writer's journal. *See* Journal.
Writing routine, 17–20, 21–23
Wylie, Elinor, 240–241

Zinsser, William, 187

(**ACKNOWLEDGMENTS** continued from page 2.)

Enstad. Reprinted, courtesy of the Chicago Tribune./ "Here—Hold My Hand" by Mari Evans. From I AM A BLACK WOMAN, published by William Morrow and Company, 1970, by permission of the author./ From GOLDFINGER by Ian Fleming. Copyright © 1959 Glidrose Productions Ltd. Reprinted by permission of the Macmillan Publishing Co., Inc., and Jonathan Cape Ltd./ "Acquainted with the Night," "Fireflies in the Garden," two lines from "A Minor Bird" by Robert Frost. From THE POETRY OF ROBERT FROST, edited by Edward Connery Lathem. Copyright 1928, © 1969 by Holt, Rinehart and Winston. Copyright © 1956 by Robert Frost. Reprinted by permission of Holt, Rinehart and Winston, Publishers./ "Nikki-Roasa" by Nikki Giovanni. From BLACK JUDGEMENT. Copyright © 1968, by Nikki Giovanni. Reprinted by permission of Broadside Press./ From "La Dolce Viva" by Barbara Goldsmith. Copyright © 1968 by the NYM Corp. Reprinted with the permission of NEW YORK Magazine./ From "DePaul Law Students Pass Supreme Test" by Peter Gorner. Reprinted, courtesy of the Chicago Tribune./ From "No Answer" by William Hanley, from Collision Course, edited by Edward Parone. Copyright 1968 by William Hanley. Reprinted by permission of Random House, Inc./ From A RAISIN IN THE SUN by Lorraine Hansberry. Copyright 1959 by Lorraine Hansberry. Reprinted by permission of Random House, Inc./ "Those Winter Sundays" by Robert Hayden. From SELECTED POEMS. Copyright © 1966 by Robert Hayden. Reprinted by permission of October House./ From Toys in the Attic by Lillian Hellman. Copyright 1959 by Lillian Hellman. Reprinted by permission of Random House, Inc./ Reprinted by permission of Charles Scribner's Sons from "The Killers" (copyright 1927 Charles Scribner's Sons) by Ernest Hemingway from MEN WITHOUT WOMEN./ From "On the Blue Water" by Ernest Hemingway. Copyright by Ernest Hemingway 1936. Copyright © renewed by Mary Hemingway 1964. First published in Esquire Magazine./ From "The Short Happy Life of Francis Macomber" (copyright 1936 Ernest Hemingway) from THE SHORT STORIES OF ERNEST HEM-INGWAY and from "The Three-Day Blow" (copyright 1925 Charles Scribner's Sons) from IN OUR TIME, both by Ernest Hemingway. Reprinted by permission of Charles Scribner's Sons / "Legend" by Patricia Irving from THE WHISPERING WIND, edited by Terry Allen. Copyright © 1972 by The Institute of American Indian Arts. Reprinted by permission of Doubleday & Company, Inc./ From Jack Kerouac's unpublished private journal; owned by the University of Texas Humanities Research Center; copyright © 1949 by Jack Kerouac. Reprinted by permission of The Sterling Lord Agency, Inc./ "What Were They Like?" by Denise Levertov. From THE SORROW DANCE. Copyright © 1966 by Denise Levertov Goodman. Reprinted by permission of New Directions Publishing Corporation./ Ken Lohmann's poem "Tortoise" and Mark R. Brown's poem "Cat!" appeared originally in A.L. Lazarus, ed., The IAC POETS–IN–THE–SCHOOLS issue, SPARROW 30, 1974, published by Felix and Selma Stefanile through a grant from the Indiana Arts Commission and the USOE./ From THE CRUCIBLE by Arthur Miller, copyright 1952, 1953 by Arthur Miller. Reprinted by permission of The Viking Press./ "Song of the Open Road" from VERSES FROM 1929 ON by Ogden Nash. Copyright 1932 by Ogden Nash. This poem originally appeared in The New Yorker. Used by permission of Little, Brown and Co./ From THE PASSPORT by Saul Steinberg. Reprinted by permission of Julian Bach Literary Agency. Copyright © 1954 by Saul Steinberg./ "Words on a Windy Day" from NOTES FOR A GUIDEBOOK by Lucien Stryk, copyright 1965, published by The Swallow Press Incorporated./ "For Witches" by Susan Sutheim. Copyright 1969 by Women: A Journal of Liberation, 3028 Green-mount Avenue, Baltimore, Maryland 21218./ From "Petrified Man" and "A Visit of Charity" from A CURTAIN OF GREEN AND OTHER STORIES by Eudora Welty. Copyright 1941 by Eudora Welty. Reprinted by permission of Harcourt Brace Jovanovich, Inc./ "Complete Destruction" by William Carlos Williams. From COLLECTED EARLIER POEMS. Copyright 1938 by New Directions Publishing Corporation. Reprinted by permission of New Directions Publishing Corporation./ From THE KANDY-KOLORED TANGERINE-FLAKE STREAMLINE BABY by Tom Wolfe. Copyright © 1963, 1964, 1965 by Thomas K. Wolfe, Jr., copyright © 1963, 1964, 1965 by New York Herald Tribune, Inc. Reprinted with the permission of Farrar, Straus & Giroux, Inc./ From "Pop Therapy: Woody Allen" from POP GOES AMERCIA by William K. Zinsser, published by Harper & Row, 1966. Reprinted by permission of the author.